MOBILIS
POWER O
YOU KNOW

MOBILISING THE POWER OF WHAT YOU KNOW

A PRACTICAL GUIDE TO SUCCESSFUL KNOWLEDGE MANAGEMENT

Paul Miller

Research by
Mehul Bakrania

CENTURY
BUSINESS

First published in 1998 by Century Ltd
Random House, 20 Vauxhall Bridge Road, London SW1V 2SA

Random House Australia (Pty) Limited
20 Alfred Street, Milsons Point
Sydney, New South Wales 2061, Australia

Random House New Zealand Limited
18 Poland Road, Glenfield
Auckland 10, New Zealand

Random House South Africa (Pty) Limited
Endulini, 5a Jubilee Road, Parktown 2193, South Africa

Random House UK Limited Reg. No. 954009

Papers used by Random House UK Limited are natural, recyclable
products made from wood grown in sustainable forests. The
manufacturing processes conform to the environmental
regulations of the country of origin.

Typeset by SX Composing DTP, Rayleigh, Essex
Printed by Mackays of Chatham plc, Chatham, Kent

ISBN 0 7126 7913 8

Companies, institutions and other organizations wishing to make
bulk purchases of any business books published by Random House
should contact their local bookstore or Random House direct:

Special Sales Director
Random House, 20 Vauxhall Bridge Road, London SW1V 2SA
Tel 0171 840 8470   Fax 0171 828 6681

ww.randomhouse.co.uk
businessbooks@randomhouse.co.uk

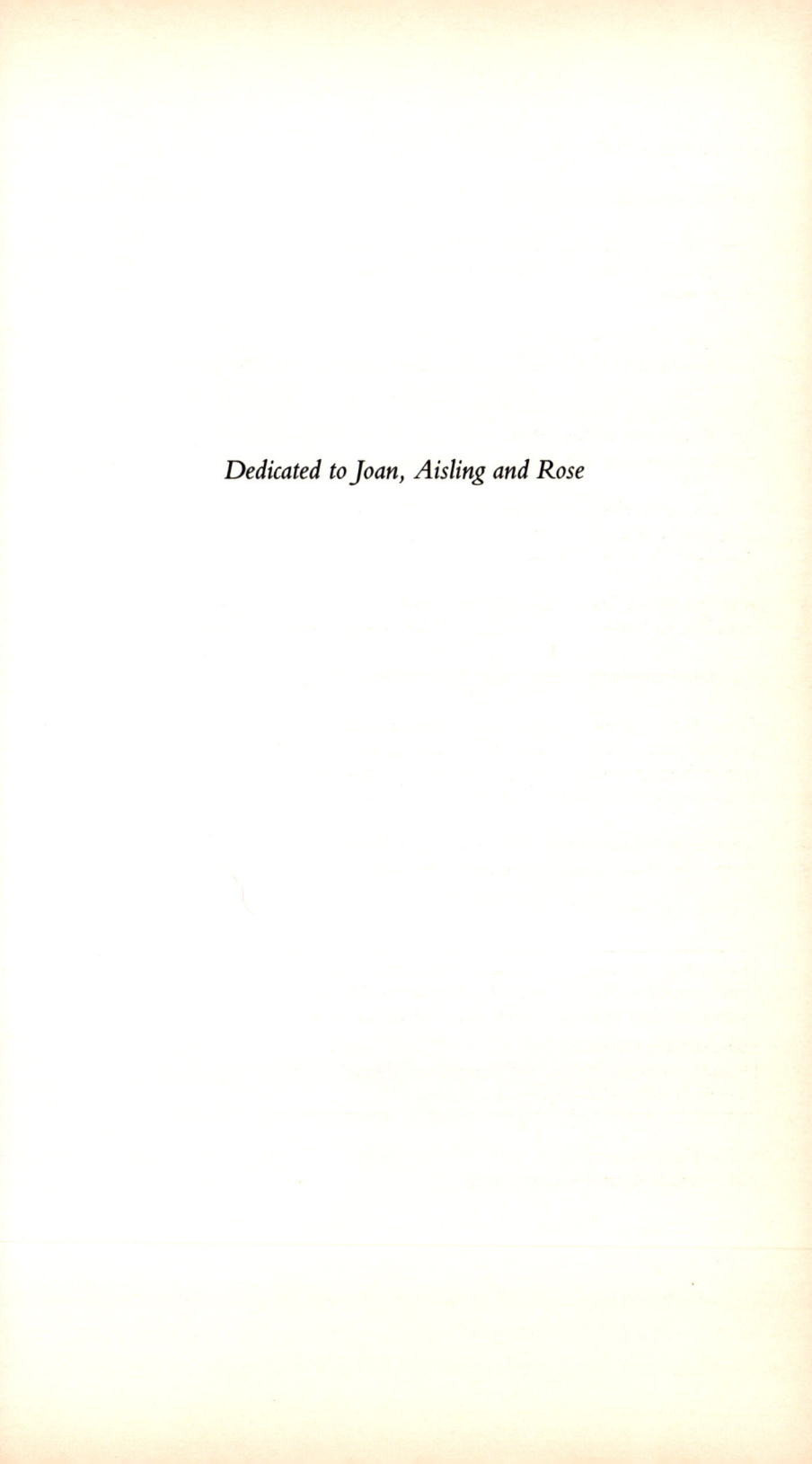

Dedicated to Joan, Aisling and Rose

Acknowledgements

Special thanks to Amy Anderson, Anna Paul, Lynn Fraser, Helen Cannon, Amanda Brooks and all at TEG. Thanks also to Mehul Bakrania for his invaluable research and to Penny Klein who carried out a UK survey into knowledge mobilisation. Thanks also to our clients and contributors who have made this project possible.

Contents

1.
Introduction

IF ONLY WE COULD HARNESS IT ALL . . .

On any given day, in a large organisation, there are many people working on the same problem – duplicating work, re-inventing the wheel or, worst of all, failing to use what the organisation already knows.

For years, senior management have been saying: 'People are our greatest asset,' without really meaning it. Certainly, people are the key to the traditional areas where people matter, such as customer service, quality and relationships. More importantly, however, they are also the 'containers' of everything that any organisation – large or small – knows. It is starting to dawn on senior management that knowledge really can be power, that mobilising what you – as an organisation – know can produce a new level of organisational strength and competitive edge.

People are the key

This was perfectly expressed in a recent advertising campaign by the global broking firm, Merrill Lynch. Over a collage of shots of its people in distant locations, the voice-over declared that when using Merrill Lynch you don't get one Merrill Lynch banker, you get the collected knowledge and wisdom of all Merrill Lynch employees world-wide, with their 40-plus years of experience. It's a powerful and attractive idea. I'm sure the company has made progress in mobilising its knowledge, but it is still a holy grail for Merrill Lynch (as for all its competitors) rather than a daily reality.

The motivation for this book is to give you, the reader, a practical handbook on what has so far been an esoteric and rather academic subject. Perhaps you have heard a little about this strange-sounding topic of knowledge management, but have found that much that is written is abstract, conceptual or too technology-led? This book attempts to give a down-to-earth guide to knowledge management (or, for reasons explained in the next section, what I choose to call knowledge mobilisation), from a European viewpoint since, up to now, most of the literature and articles have been mainly US-focused.

This book is based on my own and my colleagues' experience at UK-based internal communication consultancy TEG, gathered 'at the coalface' during many projects that have tried to draw out, capture and share what large companies know. It is not an exact science and probably never will be. What organisations know is as difficult to pin down as the collected knowledge of humanity – scattered, constantly evolving, often hidden, and only partly capable of being documented. Knowledge is the kind of subject that makes business managers nervous - important but elusive.

'Seizing the opportunity now' is a real possibility

Think about this! Each day, every person in your company arrives 'carrying' everything they know. Wouldn't it be great if, when person A is working, he or she could somehow dip into the knowledge of every other person in the company and apply it to his/her own work? Put like that, you might well ask why it has taken so long for companies to realise this enormous potential. There are a myriad factors which make knowledge management an important, current need. These include the arrival of truly global markets, flatter organisations and an ever-greater need for competitive edge.

A simpler answer could be that the time for knowledge has arrived because, for the first time ever, the communication technology is now available to enable companies to identify, capture and share at least some of what they know. This has made 'seizing the opportunity now' a real possibility.

If you can hook people together by using telephones, e-mail, intranets/internets, faxes, video conferencing, shared networks, global meetings and conferences, job rotation and easy air travel, then mobilising the power of what you know becomes achievable. Was it not the case that when the technology for space exploration became attainable, then talk of putting a man on the moon moved from science fiction to science forecast?

'Doing' things is not the future – 'knowing' things is

My own awareness of 'knowledge' as a subject of importance for organisations began in 1985 when, as a business journalist, I was fortunate enough to interview Peter Drucker, regarded by many as the world's most influential management writer and thinker. I managed to spend a working week in his company and what struck me – apart from his ability to enthral a small group of senior managers for days at a time without any 'props'– was his fervent belief that only those organisations with true 'knowledge-based' people could survive commercially. For him, knowledge was the only sustainable edge any company could have. 'Doing' things was not the future – 'knowing' things was.

For the managers who listened to Drucker this was adopted as an incontrovertible truth, but what, they asked, could they do in response? At that time, neither Drucker nor those managers knew clearly what a 'knowledge-based business' looked like, but the arrival of knowledge management in the nineties comes from the views and debate initiated by Drucker; it answers some of the questions with which those (and countless other) managers have struggled.

Time To Mobilise Knowledge – Not Manage It

One of the other spurs to writing this book was my frustration – not only at the endless conceptual talk about 'intellectual capital, knowledge assets, and knowledge-based business', but at the term 'knowledge management' itself. It sounds so dry, so dull. Also, by talking of 'management', an illusion is created that this huge and nebulous thing called knowledge can somehow be managed in the same way that a company's pay and benefits systems can be managed. It's a contradiction in terms. Knowledge can not be managed in any strict sense – particularly in an internet world – rather what businesses want to do with knowledge is to use it, share it, develop it – and mobilise it!

In fact, we at TEG had been working with clients for two years on what I now call knowledge mobilisation projects without any of us (clients or consultants) realising that we were involved in pioneering work in the field of 'knowledge management'. Our clients (senior line managers in global businesses) wouldn't have understood the term if they had heard it, but my goodness, did they have a clear grasp of the importance of sharing great ideas, concepts, applications and experiences across their business.

> *'Knowledge management' sounds dry, but is actually saturated with energy and vigour*

People who run an organisation want to get hold of its collective knowledge, wisdom and understanding so that they can really use it during every customer interaction, new product meeting, process improvement, brand development and the like. They want the passion, energy and dynamism that comes from mobilising the power of what their organisation knows.

'Knowledge management', conveys a static, inert and uninspiring message and I believe that this image has damaged the field in several ways. It has allowed the process to be taken hostage by management theorists, academics and technology firms. The term 'knowledge management' has always been difficult to explain because it lacks clarity and, worst of all, it sounds dry when it is actually saturated with energy and vigour. What companies want to do is mobilise the power of what they know – they want to mobilise everything their people know. For this reason, I talk about knowledge mobilisation throughout the book.

What I have done is to trawl through my day-to-day experiences when working with companies to look for stories of knowledge being successfully managed – in other words, shared with others. The reassuring news is that the best approaches and most effective solutions are those that are simple and practical. There are numerous theories, models and concepts of knowledge management which run parallel to the stories of progress companies have made in achieving a degree of knowledge mobilisation, but knowledge mobilisation is, in the end, a practical activity.

This book is a corporate handbook about how to share what you know. It is based on experience gained working with managers who shared the 'knowledge vision', and from numerous interviews with people and companies who have charted some ground themselves.

Enjoy your journey and share your success!

2.
What Are We Talking About?

It is in many ways unfortunate that the field of knowledge management contains such an abstract and cerebral term as 'knowledge'. Managers like things they can get their hands on and 'knowledge' doesn't sound like one of them. Many people have tried to introduce a better term, but without success. To me the alternatives sometimes offered, 'intellectual assets' or 'intellectual capital', are deepening the problem of understanding, not resolving it. So let's start by deciding what knowledge is in the first place.

The Lessons Of History

The first and most obvious thing to say is that knowledge is nothing new. Human history is in many ways a chronicle of increasing knowledge. In fact, knowledge is often what we treasure most from our history. Looking back at the great civilisations, such as the Roman, Egyptian and Greek empires, what we value most from them is the knowledge they developed and passed on. Whether it was knowledge of how to construct cities, understanding of mathematics or astronomy, it is what those cultures knew that stands the test of time. It is the legacy we remember.

Knowledge is often what we treasure most from history

There are many lessons for organisations from the experience of civilisations with knowledge. After all, organisations are mini versions of civilisations; groupings of people bound together through a shared sense of identity who attempt to advance in a general direction, be it economic, social or geographical. Think of any well-known company and we think of a distinct entity. It is interesting to ask ourselves what it is about companies such as Sony, Mercedes-Benz or Mars that customers really value. They will talk about the products or services but, in the end, isn't it the collective expertise, experience and the knowledge that those giants have that we are buying?

When a giant company dies or just struggles for a while, people talk of what it developed and what it knew. For example, we had conversations about IBM during its dark days in the late eighties and early nineties: 'But IBM put a PC on every desk – how could it fail?' That was IBM's legacy or, put another way, that was IBM's collective knowledge applied to its marketplace. If we each think about our own organisations from that high ground, and ask ourselves what our company's legacy would be if it disappeared tomorrow, we will be led to the most valuable things our company knows.

A chief legacy of ancient Rome was the knowledge the Romans developed about underground heating, sewerage and transport. That expertise provided a means to expand the Roman powerbase geographically. In the same way, when a company builds knowledge in a particular area it is with an end in mind: for instance if we accumulate knowledge about the way shoppers absorb information when they enter our stores, we can then adapt our store layouts to respond to that. From the grand to the mundane, perhaps, as an analogy, but the common thread is that knowledge is gathered for a purpose.

We value communication – the ability to link ourselves
together

It is fascinating to consider how often the leaps in knowledge which have the most impact have been associated with inventions that help people communicate more easily, more quickly, more powerfully or in entirely new ways. Think of the printing press, the telephone, television and the personal computer. We value most the knowledge about how to improve our communication – our ability to link ourselves together.

This leads to a further observation about knowledge that anyone considering knowledge mobilisation within their company should keep in mind. 'Knowledge is power' is a familiar cliché that nonetheless captures an important truth. In many periods, nations and organisations, knowledge has been the path to power at a fundamental level.

Look at any authoritarian regime and you will find the suppression of knowledge. Hitler burnt books that contained knowledge that threatened his world view. The Soviet Union controlled the media, publishing and even local communication between people; a regime grew in which people were fearful to talk to their neighbours. In Cambodia, Pol Pot destroyed the country's history, returning the people to what he called 'Year Zero', by attempting to wipe out the nation's memory. In a revolution, the first place to be seized is the radio or television centre – the means of sharing knowledge. In China, the Cultural Revolution sought to wipe out all artistic expression, along with the more typical forms of suppression of knowledge. In the apartheid times of South Africa, the divisive system was kept in place by creating a climate in which no one could openly question apartheid; the knowledge of alternatives was buried.

The point these examples illustrate is that knowledge has

always been a source of power, and the more authoritarian approaches have been the most threatened by it when it is left unregulated. If we go back to the start of the twentieth century, it would be difficult to find many organisations that did not manage knowledge in the company by attempting to control and hoard it. Probably the first large business to challenge this 'knowledge secrecy' was IBM which, by 1940, was already beginning to develop pioneering internal communication approaches which have influenced the way companies communicate internally across the board.

Where would you rank your company on a scale of knowledge secrecy/ knowledge openness?

When you attempt to gather and share knowledge in your organisation you may find that you are mounting a profound and painful challenge to the way knowledge is regarded. Don't be alarmed by that. Remember that your company's view is not an isolated one, but one born out of history. That is no reason not to attempt to mobilise knowledge, but it should induce a clear respect for the size of the task in some businesses.

Understanding Knowledge

So now, to understand what knowledge is, let's start by describing what it isn't. There are many ways of classifying knowledge but, having studied many of them, I find the most suitable is to talk of four elements in any business: data, information, knowledge and wisdom.

What Is Data?

At its most basic level, data is a structured set of records of transactions. All the names and details of customers of a bank is data. If someone debits their account by £100, the banks knows when, where and how that transaction took place. It doesn't know why the money was extracted or why the person chose that branch for the transaction. This type of data is typically held in a database or data management system. It accumulates constantly so most organisations have become adept at data management. Data has no intrinsic meaning or value; it is neutral.

What Is Information?

Peter Drucker said that information is 'data endowed with relevance and purpose'. By this he means that it is one step up the evolutionary ladder from data. Information always contains some data but it also contains a message. The verb 'to inform' means 'to give shape to' at its root. Information usually comes in written, audible or visible form and will have a sender and a receiver. It is up to the receiver to decide if what they get is information or just data. The sender may think they have sent information, but it may not communicate itself to the receiver.

Information is one step up the evolutionary ladder from data
If all the bank's branch transactions for one week are categorised, added up to give an overall picture of money movements, compared to other weeks/branches, summarised and sent to the branch manager, what the manager receives is information; it has form and meaning. It is fair to say that some organisations have made great advances in this area in the past ten years and managers are often well informed about some areas of their business, typically financial areas. However, on the flip side, how many of us have complained about 'information overload' and being swamped by e-mail we don't want or need?

What Is Knowledge?

As said above, what we value from the great civilisations of history is their knowledge. Knowing facts about ancient China is interesting, but the teaching of Chinese philosophy has meaning for how we live today – that knowledge we remember. We can also recall the teacher at school who not only knew the facts about great poets, but had a real understanding of particular poets and their motivations and concerns. Somehow we know that knowledge means far more than the contents of the latest FYI message on our desks. We talk of knowledgeable people, knowledge-rich companies and we have an impression of intelligence, education and experience.

Knowledge is more than the contents of an FYI message

In the context of our bank example, if the bank decided to interview a cross-section of staff and customers, to analyse trends over a period of a year across certain branches, and then to gather what it had learnt into a handbook on best practice customer retention or cross-selling, that output would be knowledge. It would draw on the professional experience of bank employees, the attitudes of their customers and an informed analysis of what is happening across its branch network.

As can be seen in taking the bank example further, when we talk about knowledge the situation becomes more and more complex. For that reason I will not attempt an endless definition, but talk instead about the components of knowledge. Knowledge can exist in many forms and cannot be easily described since it draws on the experience of people, insights they have, changing business practices and the wealth of documentation in all forms that exists. One way that knowledge has been described is: 'If it isn't data or information but is really helpful, it is likely to be knowledge.'

One interesting aspect of knowledge is that it can only be developed (so far) by people. While technology can generate data and, to some extent, information, knowledge requires human intervention to make comparisons, draw out implications and relationships between bits of information, and discuss the information with others.

Information moves fast – knowledge takes time

SmithKline Beecham, for example, decided it needed to document what it knew about its most successful brands. It did so through a series of global brand guides which were then sent to all markets world-wide. In most cases, the guides took the best part of a year to compile because of the numbers of people, experiences and stories that needed to be gathered and sorted. Information can come fast – knowledge takes time. Colgate operates a similar system with 'bundle books' that are kept current through updates. They are not perfectly designed but they follow a set structure and use consistent language that brand managers recognise.

It is worth saying that one form of knowledge that has been highlighted in the last few years as having clear business value is 'best practice'. A business's best practices are one type of knowledge in the minds of an organisation's people. The SmithKline Beecham and Colgate experiences are to do with sharing the type of knowledge we call best practice. It is interesting to note that best practice has often been an organisation's route into knowledge mobilisation. Usually the story goes like this: a team at Boeing or Ford or Honda develops a new product or product feature in a way that is noticeably different from the way things are normally done. Its development time is considerably less than normal or it costs considerably less; the senior managers notice this and say, 'How did those guys do that? Let's find out and tell everyone else to do the same thing!'

'Best practice' has a clear business value

The development of the Ford Saturn car was a prime example of sharing best practice. Teams working on the new vehicle decided to work in parallel (rather than sequentially) and the lead time was reduced massively. A team in Ford studied the 'recipe', documented it and then shared what Ford recognised to be best practice. Knowledge of value in an organisation comes in many forms, but many companies have experienced best practice sharing at some level. Few companies are really new to knowledge mobilisation.

Best practice is only one type of knowledge. There are many – but you have to name them to know them and not all organisational knowledge is worth knowing. A company may have a great deal of knowledge about shipping because, as a manufacturer of fridges, it has to ship products to many locations. However, spending energy identifying, capturing and sharing that knowledge is not useful to the company as a whole. It is sufficient that the handful of people in the company who carry out the task retain and update that area of knowledge themselves.

Identify knowledge that is relevant and worthy of mobilisation
In contrast to shipping, knowledge of evolving consumer trends in different countries that are likely to impact on fridge use in the next ten years is more widely valuable. It is useful for people at many points in the company – market research, R&D, marketing, sales, finance etc – and so is worth mobilising. The best place to start is to identify knowledge you have that is relevant and worthy of mobilisation. It can come in strange forms; many Japanese companies will routinely collect development ideas and concepts that failed to become products on the basis that they could spark future successful ideas.

Some knowledge is harder to grasp than others. When long-serving employees leave, a great deal of 'tacit' knowledge – knowledge that is hidden from view which even the individuals themselves cannot describe – will leave with them, despite the new emerging practice of exit interviews which are taped and archived. For a sales manager, this might be the knowledge or instinct, born of experience, about what to do in tricky negotiations for new accounts. This knowledge can be assessed against the fifty terrific business generation ideas that worked which that individual pioneered in the past five years; these ideas could then at least be shared (and often used) by sales managers working in 25 other countries.

HARD	EASY
tacit	explicit
hidden	visible
undocumented	documented
unstructured	ordered
complex	simple

Knowledge can be easy or hard to capture

It is not that the harder types of knowledge should be ignored, but it is vital to notice what kind of knowledge you are trying to capture. Starting with the 'easier' areas is sensible because there are more quick wins and the growing pains are less severe. We will talk more about this later.

What Is Wisdom?

If knowledge is hard to pin down, wisdom is even harder. Most discussion of knowledge avoids the topic, but it is important. If we assume that, over the next twenty years, organisations make as much progress with knowledge mobilisation as they have with data and information management, then the next frontier will be capturing the collective wisdom of the company and laying that at the service of the customer, as the Merrill Lynch commercial mentioned in Chapter 1 implies.

The next frontier is to capture the collective wisdom of the company

Wisdom is the stuff of mythology – King Arthur and his wizard Merlin, Homer's *Iliad* or (in more contemporary form) the *Star Wars* films. At times, business leaders apply it in powerful ways to steer their people in new directions. Was it not wisdom at work that allowed Sony to see the possibility of a miniature cassette player that you could carry in your pocket? Suffice it to say that all organisations develop wisdom after a reasonable history of trading and it can be a resource for the business if it is allowed to express itself.

So What Is Knowledge Mobilisation?

Whether you call it knowledge sharing, knowledge mobilisation or knowledge management, few people can explain precisely what this new business movement is actually about. Most senior managers know that mobilising knowledge has been billed as a critical tool for the twenty-first-century corporation. They know it's the subject of books, magazine articles, conferences, business school classes and World Wide Web sites. They may even have people on the headcount with responsibility for knowledge.

Experts disagree on what to call the collective efforts to capture, organise and share what employees know. Some talk of 'managing intellectual capital', others of 'capitalising on intellectual assets' or 'harnessing knowledge resources'. Confusion is natural. Mobilising knowledge is new, sounds important, and is difficult to pin down to hard facts and data deliverables. I read one definition (admittedly of knowledge management) that brings out the best and worst in the subject: 'Knowledge management is the systematic approach to increasing the value of the knowledge capital of your organisation to enable change and community building.' This came from Andersen Consulting and, while it contains a lot of good stuff, try delivering that to a board of directors with short attention spans. It is loaded with concepts and vague language; it even fails to communicate what the topic is – rather ironic, given that it seeks to define what knowledge sharing is all about.

Maximise the capabilities of your people by capturing their expertise

If our goal is to mobilise the power of what a business knows, then everything we do in pursuit of that goal should 'model' the new culture and climate. All talk should be clear, direct and easy to understand. It should be easy for people at all levels of the organisation to understand what knowledge mobilisation is and how to put it into practice. It should not threaten people by seeming too esoteric and should be grounded in practicality at all times.

Knowledge mobilisation represents the attempts of organisations to maximise the capabilities of their people by capturing their expertise and turning it into a corporate asset by sharing it. This is only possible in organisations that view their knowledge as important.

Most devotees agree about why it is important. Increasingly, in organisations 'you are what you know', and a company that 'knows' more today than it did yesterday is a company with more expertise, knowledge and understanding to sell. In fact, due to downsizing, frequent job jumping, constant organisational change, globalisation etc, companies feel more pressure than ever to maintain a well-informed workforce and hence gain competitive advantage.

3.
Why Is Knowledge Mobilisation Important?

Why Is Interest In Knowledge Mobilisation Growing?

Today's managers have access to more information than ever. They can visit websites, tap into databases and call on corporate expertise by using their company's internal networks.

It is easy to confuse information technology with information
The problem, as Peter Drucker says, is that it is easy to confuse data with knowledge, or information technology with information. As ever-increasing volumes of data become available, the difficulty of sifting, mobilising and exploiting it has become ever more acute.

In response, the business community has a new breed of managers who go by titles such as 'Chief Knowledge Officer', 'Chief Learning Officer', 'Director of Intellectual Capital' or 'Director of Intellectual Asset Management'. At least a dozen major companies, including Andersen Consulting, Coca-Cola,

Monsanto, General Electric, Coopers and Lybrand and Skandia, have created this role in the past three years.

These are often senior positions with broad responsibilities. Take Ellen Knapp, Chief Knowledge Officer of Coopers and Lybrand (now Price Waterhouse Coopers). She is a vice-chairperson, a member of the management committee and is also on the board of partners. She is responsible for all aspects of the firm's technology, learning, education and market analysis. As Ellen says: 'The job of the Chief Knowledge Officer is to create, use, retain and transfer knowledge. That is not just data, but the intellectual capital that is in people's minds and published work.'

Knapp is typical of many of this first wave of knowledge mobilisation in that she has a technological background. It is natural that IT people begin the process as this gives companies a sense that their new knowledge mobilisation initiatives are grounded in something solid – technology. However, as we will see later, the heart of successful knowledge mobilisation does not lie in the technology (though it is an essential pathway) but in the motivation of people to participate and the processes they follow.

For the IT people, their new jobs have been extended to include issues such as training skills, incentives and strategy. As Michael Earl, Professor of Information Management at the London Business School, says: 'As knowledge involves more than IT, companies feel they need to have someone in a co-ordinating role to pull the different aspects of human resources, IT and strategy together.'

Such new jobs highlight a widespread view that there is a gap in expertise at board level. When KPMG's senior managers recently examined this issue as part of a programme on inform-ation management, they found that: 'Whilst most boards feel comfortable with most subjects on the agenda – financial, marketing, personnel, business strategy – information manage-ment is considered difficult.' The KPMG group, chaired by Robert Hawley, Chief Executive of British Energy, also found that neglect of these issues could have disastrous consequences.

It cited numerous examples of failure, ranging from the leak of a bank's credit screening system to a heavy fine imposed on a company because it was unable to produce records of employee training.

The group also found examples where successful information management had brought notable rewards. Information technology allowed one company to win more contracts by combining detailed information across its organisation and between its suppliers to achieve faster and more accurate bids. Another was able to improve the design of goods and components by logging and monitoring component failures. The conclusion of the Hawley group was that boards of directors should address their responsibilities for information assets in the same way as for other assets, such as property or plant.

Companies only use a small fraction of their company's knowledge

A similar argument is made by Charles Handy, the UK management writer, who points out that no executive would leave factory space or cash idle, yet companies frequently confess that they use only a small fraction of their company's knowledge. 'The emerging importance of intellectual property, broadly defined, is going to change many things beyond recognition,' he says.

Skandia has already tackled the issue. It argues that the gap between the market value of a company and its book value implies that there are 'huge hidden values that are not visible in traditional accounting'. It has tried to create a systematic method of accounting for and managing its intellectual capital, which it defines as the competence and capabilities of its employees, together with databases, software manuals, trademarks and organisational structure.

Several external issues mean that mobilising knowledge is of increasing importance to companies.

Changing work patterns accelerate the need for knowledge mobilisation

Changing work patterns have accelerated the need for knowledge mobilisation. Today more than ever, a person is unlikely to stay with one organisation all their working life. It is therefore important to maximise the skills of that employee by ensuring that they share their knowledge.

Truly diversified businesses are getting rarer, with most companies focusing themselves around one or two core business areas. This means that, as businesses get closer in their markets or offerings, the opportunity for mobilising knowledge increases. The 'centre' or parent organisation is beginning to redefine its role as that of co-ordinator with the aim of adding value through increased productivity of its subsidiaries. This is where mobilising knowledge is seen as key to the success of the different businesses.

More and more of what people buy and sell has to do with knowledge. This fact is highlighted by the growth of, for example, management consultancy and the legal profession. Even production workers in increasingly sophisticated factories spend most of their time manipulating information or acquiring and applying expertise.

With trade barriers coming down and the potential of truly global communication, competition is increasing and new competitors are entering what were traditionally 'secure' markets. Companies are recognising the need to compete on a global scale and share the knowledge they have, to create a competitive advantage. They are realising that it is the organisation and not the individual who competes and therefore must pool all resources.

Technology has made knowledge mobilisation feasible on a global scale

Technology has created channels for mobilising knowledge that did not exist before. It has also changed the economies of mobilising information; today it is just as cost-effective to share knowledge between ten or ten-thousand workers.

Is It Just A Passing Management Trend, Or Here For The Long Run?

Mobilising knowledge is a popular topic at present. It is being heralded as the latest vehicle for creating sustainable competitive advantage. Companies are responding to the issue by investing in it and hiring knowledge professionals. This interest is fired by the fact that changing work patterns have resulted in a high turnover of staff who take knowledge with them. Also, technology has made mobilising knowledge feasible on a global basis and more of what companies sell is knowledge-based.

> *Knowledge mobilisation is the latest vehicle for creating competitive advantage*

The evidence for this interest is a plethora of articles, conferences and company projects. Does this indicate a radical change in the way businesses are run, or is mobilising knowledge simply the latest management money spinner? It is certain that many companies are investing heavily in knowledge mobilisation and seeing early, modest but tangible results. This in itself suggests that companies cannot afford to avoid the issue.

There are now many conferences that prove beyond doubt that the management of intellectual resources, which began almost ten years ago, has now reached a critical mass of insight. More and more experts from many disciplines are exploring and defining new management practices for capitalising on a knowledge-based economy. Consultancies believe that interest is spreading throughout industry. Ellen Knapp is convinced that knowledge mobilisation and the role of the Chief Knowledge Officer will become important for manufacturers who need to get closer to their customers, just as do the professional services companies.

Companies will try to differentiate themselves through knowledge
Knapp goes as far as stating that, as we become clearer about the pace of transition from the industrial economy to the knowledge economy, the Chief Knowledge Officer will become a very prominent role for a senior executive in many organisations. She believes that companies will increasingly try to differentiate themselves through knowledge, rather than financial capital or natural resources. Knowledge is being asserted as a new source of competitive advantage.

As the information age unfolds, more and more of what people buy, sell and do has knowledge as its raw material. Think of the NBA graduate in Finance, who leaves business school with detailed and specific knowledge of mergers and acquisitions in the EU, with all its underlying regulatory and business implications; think of production workers at sophisticated factories who spend most of their time manipulating information or acquiring and applying expertise, not toting barges and lifting bales.

Corporate knowledge is hard to find and can disappear without trace.
Unlike traditional raw material – which is inspected, warehoused, bar-coded, and audited – corporate knowledge is scattered, hard to find and prone to disappear without a trace. If these scattered bodies of knowledge can be brought together, then the people who use them can work faster and better. Says Charles Paulk, CIO of Andersen Consulting: 'When one of our consultants shows up, the client should get the best of the firm, not just the best of that consultant.'

However, not everyone thinks that the role will take off. Jeff Leon, Managing Director of the information systems practice at Russell Reynolds, an executive search company, is sceptical. He thinks that the best Chief Information Officers already do the job of Chief Knowledge Officer. Moreover, many companies still have problems meeting their basic information requirements without even attempting to capture true knowledge.

Is It A Consultancy-Led Movement?

According to Michael Earl, Andersen Consulting is typical of many management consultancies in its enthusiastic embrace of knowledge management. Their interest lies partly in their heavy reliance on their own expertise and partly in the perception that the subject is growing in importance. 'The cynical view is that knowledge mobilisation is the hottest topic in this area of business and consultants may feel the need to show the way,' he says.

In one month recently, there were more than forty 'Does anyone know?' questions on Andersen Consulting's QuickMail bulletin board. These were separate from private e-mail messages, *ad hoc* questions, or others scavenging for knowledge that the organisation already had.

Paul Pedersen, a Price Waterhouse partner, succinctly sums up what everyone knows, but what few are prepared to address as a pressing concern: 'In the heat of marketing, consultants will promise that the firm has, say, established knowledge of world-class standards for logistics. And the firm does have it – but it's in your office or my briefcase, or with some guys out in California, or dispersed in all three places.

Knowledge databases are major strategic initiatives.
Price Waterhouse has, over the past two years, invested millions to pull all that knowledge together, map it and make it easy to use, turning human capital into a corporate attribute – structural intellectual capital. Carol Anne Ogdin, founder of Deep Woods Technology, a Santa Clara consulting firm, says: 'Knowledge databases are cropping up all over organisations we work with. These go far beyond handbooks, training manuals and in-house *Yellow Pages*; they are major strategic initiatives headed by senior executives who expect to change the way their companies operate.'

The consultants initially led the way in the turbo-charged knowledge mobilisation drive – a surprise since 'consultants are famous for diagnosing scratched corneas in their clients' peepers despite cataracts in their own.' Andersen Consulting has its Knowledge Xchange; Arthur Andersen has AA Online; Booz Allen and Hamilton has developed Knowledge On-Line (KOL); Ernst & Young has created a Centre for Business Knowledge; KPMG has a Knowledge Manager.

Booz Allen's KOL saves the company long and costly hours repeating each other's work, or re-inventing the wheel. It is easy to 'tap' experts and ideas regardless of geography or speciality. Thus a consultant in Indonesia helping an oil company improve customer service might want to crib from colleagues in Caracas or Houston, or adapt work a New Yorker did for a bank. All the consultant needs to tap into KOL is his laptop and a phone line.

Thomas W. Malone, a leading professor from MIT, states, 'We're in something of an information jungle. Survival techniques that worked in the old information deserts that we all worked in will not be as effective. Therefore, those who learn to take advantage of this increasing amount of information economically will be much more successful.'

The main conclusion from all available sources is that this is indeed a journey of discovery, and that no one person has all the answers. To establish a solid foundation for the future of intellectual capital, a collective degree of research would seem both wise and necessary.

Where Knowledge Mobilisation Fits In

Some would ask, since knowledge mobilisation is yet another business trend, how does it relate to other 'people' trends past and present, such as empowerment, best practice, quality, re-engineering and teamwork?

Drawing out trends is not an exact science, but the key business shift was the arrival of the 'quality' movement of the late seventies and early eighties. What this did was to highlight the fact not only that customers needed to receive quality products but, more importantly, that the essential component in delivering quality was the people in the business – particularly those in the front-line of production, distribution, processing etc. If your people understood what quality meant, then you could start to raise product or service standards.

Until then, it had been believed that people were 'tools' of delivery rather than 'assets' as they came to be described. Take the classic story of the car manufacturers. In the West, the quality of the cars leaving the factories was poor; often new car owners would return vehicles due to some immediate fault. Then, Japanese car makers arrived with something new: cars that were reliable because they were checked and re-checked by (who would have believed it?) the people who built them. This was the arrival of Total Quality Management and it put the onus of responsibility for quality with those 'lowest' down the organisation.

TQM was a fundamental movement as it allowed the trends that followed – best practice, empowerment, re-engineering and teamwork – to take place. These later developments maintain the premise that your people have a key role in delivering what your customers want. To do this they need to be informed, have the power to take actions, alter business processes where appropriate and work in teams to share ideas.

People with knowledge cannot help but take responsibility
In our car example, it all seems so obvious now that to have cars leave the factory in superb condition is vital, and that this must involve those who build the cars doing their jobs in a thorough and proven way. Empowerment fell naturally out of the quality movement as it involved pushing decision-making down the business, not only where quality was concerned but in many other areas of service and production.

When Xerox gave the staff in its high-street copy shops freedom to settle customer complaints up to the value of £100, this empowerment was an extension of Nissan allowing its automobile manufacturing teams to raise and implement quality improvements without involving anyone more senior than a team supervisor.

As new trends emerge, the previous trend is not dropped but is absorbed into how an organisation works; it is often incorporated into the new, more encompassing movement that follows it. So it is with knowledge mobilisation. It is a natural outcome of quality, teamwork, empowerment and best practice since all those movements demand new levels of knowledge being available to staff. At First Direct, the innovative UK telephone banking service, telesales staff have access on screen to considerable amounts of data and knowledge about the customer they are talking to. This knowledge enables them to deliver the service their customer expects and it has given them a sustained competitive advantage.

How can you empower someone but not give them the knowledge they require to be empowered? Says Jan Carlson, former head of SAS Airlines: 'An individual without knowledge cannot take responsibility; an individual with knowledge cannot help but take responsibility.' Viewed in this way, the knowledge mobilisation movement is a clear extension from empowerment and, in many ways, is a practical means of developing empowerment within a framework.

Through many knowledge mobilisation projects, I have found that the knowledge that people gain promotes new levels of ownership, responsibility and action and does so effortlessly. If you know more, you can do more.

An alternative view, which I will cite just to amuse those who carry a healthy cynicism of management consultants, is that knowledge management was an activity developed by the large consulting houses to help them share and exploit what they already knew internally, in an effort to generate more business. After seeing its value for themselves, it was offered by one or two firms to their own clients as a possible new service – behold, a new management trend and business service were born. Take your choice of which view to believe, though I believe there is truth in both versions.

4.
Is Knowledge Mobilisation For Everyone?

Since knowledge mobilisation often involves people describing their own experience to others let's start this chapter with a story from my own experience that illustrates some important features of successful knowledge sharing. It contains some general truths about knowledge mobilisation and will help us investigate whether it is useful for all types of organisations and functions.

In the early 1990s, a pharmaceuticals company noted that one of its key brands dominated in some of the 80 markets in which it was sold, but had much smaller market share in others. It identified that the reason why this fairly straightforward over-the-counter product was so successful in some markets was because the healthcare establishment – doctors, pharmacists, nurses – in those countries recommended it. The building of their trust and endorsement was called 'medical heritage'.

If developing a medical heritage was the fuel that powered the brand's success, what if the keys to building medical heritage could be learned and those practices introduced to all 80 markets?

"All managers know the 'Not Invented Here' syndrome"

When a marketing director looked across the global market, he noticed that each brand team had little or no contact with brand teams in other countries – even those close at hand geographically. Was it possible, he wondered, to export what Australia or Denmark knew to other countries? Also, if the answer to that question was yes, then how could you convince others to do similar things themselves given the 'Not Invented Here' syndrome which all managers know only too well?

After discussing this proposition with colleagues in several markets and gaining support for his ideas, he decided to trust his instinct and attempt the daunting task. Working with my own consultancy TEG, the skills, practices and know-how of a few excellent countries was captured.

Through talking to successful and unsuccessful brand teams, it was discovered that medical heritage came from novel and well-executed ideas. The successful markets built medical heritage among the healthcare profession over time through a regime of strong ideas and programmes like these. What the 80 countries really wanted was to see each great idea in its totality. Several markets contributed enthusiastically. One brand manager from Trinidad even made a semi-professional video of herself talking about work they had done with hospitals.

If you could present a visual insight into great practices from the best teams, then that might not only overcome the 'Not Invented Here' syndrome, but also give brand teams the actual knowledge they needed to put the great ideas into action locally in their own market. The question was how could what amounted to more than 200 ideas, initiatives and programmes be captured and shared quickly?

The answer was to create an internally branded communication system, comprising a printed, full-colour catalogue and a Lotus Notes database. Both the printed and electronic media contained much of the same content – stories of what brand teams had done, photographs, results and learnings and, importantly (as it turned out), contact details for the person responsible. All this was indexed for easy reference. In fact the printed catalogue was far more popular than the database because brand managers found it easier and more satisfying to learn from a printed page than a screen.

The content was tightly structured and very practical for the readers. It started out as offering the next best thing to giving every brand team a bundle of actual samples; however, when it was used, it was found to be even better than the real thing as all the content was structured, edited and organised for adaptation.

When the communication system was launched to the eighty different countries, one regional marketing director for Latin America, said it was the most useful piece of internal communication that he had seen in his 30-year career. Around 200 other managers broke into spontaneous applause at its arrival because, as one marketing director said: 'We sort of knew we understood about medical heritage as a company, but seeing it documented and so invitingly presented somehow brought that hidden knowledge into the open. You could open the catalogue and say this is what my company knows about and somebody in my business has bothered to capture this stuff and now it's all available to me.'

Numerous initiatives were sparked, some of which were direct executions of ideas pioneered by other markets. Many were adaptations of what people learned – a kind of pick-and-mix approach. Phone and e-mail contact was established between brand managers who had never met. Instead of making contact to build networks in some vague sense, the Kenyan brand manager had something specific to talk about to his Australian contact: 'Item 54 on Page 80 says . . .'. The Sri Lankan team spent a week with the Australian team and both learned how to build stronger businesses.

Knowledge is no longer something to be hoarded for career development

One question that is often asked about knowledge mobilisation is how to get people to contribute what they know – after all, isn't knowledge something you hoard as part of your career development? In the first year of the initiative, the eight best countries contributed to the communication system. Their motivation was a chance to broadcast their achievements to the global business of which they are a part. In the second year, almost 30 countries chose to contribute because the communication system had effected a change in the cultural approach of the business. Telling others about your success was viewed as a positive career move – and let's not forget that the names of the contributors went alongside every item! It became a situation where not being in the catalogue was seen to be abnormal, an indication, perhaps, that you had no good ideas to present. Peer pressure works.

Another question that is often asked is: how do you get others to apply the knowledge they learn; how do you overcome the 'Not Invented Here' syndrome? The answer will vary depending on what knowledge is being shared. In this instance, early research among brand managers showed that they were operating in markets with a long and respected history, so telling people what was best practice in a dictatorial way would provoke hostility. Instead, the format of the catalogue simply shared some interesting practical ideas; it did not tell people what to do but instead stimulated their thinking. Also, the content was helpful in areas where the users needed support. The ability to adapt locally was crucial and while there was no central policing function, the communication system was being talked about by high-level employees such as global managers, regional directors, general managers; it was seen, at a corporate level, to be important.

One small addition to each item was the name of the local brand manager and their contact details. This was added to encourage direct contact between countries, and in so doing, a subsidiary benefit was produced: a 'brand community' was developed. More brand managers and directors now know more colleagues than before and there is a tangible existence of networks and communities of people working on the brand. Overall, the brand's sales performance has improved.

The latest addition to the system, a knowledge sharing initiative about how to exploit a specific sub-brand with a CD ROM has been added to the printed book and database.

This communication system (which has won two international communication awards) demonstrates several key points:

- Choosing an area of knowledge that is of real value works
- Knowing the detailed needs of the audience is vital
- Communicating knowledge in a way that meets the needs of your audience does work
- Practical approaches are popular
- Knowledge mobilisation involves people talking, so give contact details
- Giving people an excuse to talk gets over reluctance to make contact
- Mobilising knowledge is a behavioural change – it takes time

So Is Knowledge Mobilisation For Me?

I doubt that there are many chief executives or functional heads brave enough to say, 'We don't need to share knowledge here; it's just not relevant in our industry/company/function.' That said, there are certain industries that are already ahead of others in their familiarity and involvement with knowledge mobilisation. There are also industries where knowledge sharing has more immediate use than others.

Take the media (print, radio and television), for example. Gathering and sharing data, information, knowledge and, from time to time, wisdom is what they do for a living. Every edition of the daily newspaper or television news broadcast is an output of a knowledge mobilisation process. Interestingly, the output has been refined (or edited) for relevance to its audience and many bits of knowledge will have been discarded along the way as not worthy of communication. However, media organisations (apart from their journalistic staff), in marketing, sales or finance, are no better or worse at knowledge mobilisation than other industries, despite their core skill in knowledge sharing. Even within the journalistic staff there are two standards applied to knowledge. One is a total sharing of what a staff member knows, since that is their daily job. However, the staff hold their contacts, news gathering techniques and ways of producing stories to be confidential and tacit, to be guarded from the eyes of colleagues due to a strong sense of internal competition.

Information transfer is a weapon as powerful as a missile

Then there are industries such as healthcare and science research with large research and development parts of their business which are imbued with a culture of knowledge sharing, based on the academic tradition of peer group networking. It is worth noting that it was among US academic institutions and the military that the internet was born. Universities had always shared knowledge to enhance their reputation and for reciprocal benefits. The military (particularly the US Army) saw information transfer as a weapon as powerful (and more so) than a missile. Likewise, the UK Army, as far back as 1970, in its role in Northern Ireland, believed that its intimate knowledge of terrorist activities was its main non-lethal weapon.

It is possible to say that there are industries where knowledge mobilisation is less essential than others, but it is hard to name any that do not need to address the issue at some level. For a management consultancy, mobilising knowledge is vital as without it, a key part of what it sells is not being capitalised upon. On the other hand, a furniture manufacturer may benefit from sharing knowledge, but will gain a less dramatic payback than the consultancy. At a commercial level, mobilising knowledge in areas that impact the customer strongly – such as sales, marketing and customer service – is more important than doing so within human resources.

In truth, no company can afford not to consider knowledge mobilisation. It does not have to create a Director of Knowledge or, beneath a certain size, install state-of-the-art IT, but every company should be moving towards fostering a culture that will encourage daily swapping of information, easy-to-access knowledge and a workforce that is willing to co-operate. In some respects, mobilising knowledge is not new. Many companies have been carrying it out, *ad hoc*, for years – writing handbooks, creating company directories and databases. However, to maximise the benefits of knowledge, it has to be *mobilised*.

All companies compete through the skills of their employees
In these early days, organisations in the service industry or those which are selling the 'knowledge' of its workers will gain the greatest benefit from knowledge mobilisation. The large consulting firms have invested heavily. In reality, knowledge mobilisation applies to all companies, since all companies compete through the skills of their employees. The actual management of the process is most relevant to large, multi-national companies which operate in the global marketplace. This is because they are geographically diverse and their sheer size creates detachment amongst employees. However, small companies have an advantage in the area of tacit knowledge. It is easier to transmit knowledge in this case as employees routinely observe others and work in close physical proximity.

5.
How Should We Approach Knowledge Mobilisation?

A good place to start is with the issue of motivation mentioned in the case study in Chapter 4.

What Motivates People To Mobilise Knowledge?

A frequent issue that is raised about projects like the communication system discussed in Chapter 4 is how to motivate people to participate. The thought being that knowledge mobilisation is like a 'pot luck' party where its success depends not only on everyone bringing food, but also on the quality of the food they bring. Rubbish in – rubbish out!

The Australian team members in the OTC example cited were an interesting case as they had a lot to share but not, as we thought, that much to learn. So how could we motivate them? The following payoffs for the Australians were an indication of the ingredients that lead to motivation anywhere. These are not in order of importance as different people, markets and types of companies are not influenced by the same factors and issues.

Payback

People want access to knowledge that they can benefit from
You contribute to the overall pool of knowledge because then you can draw from that pool yourself, and you never know what you might learn. It's a version of 'you scratch my back and I'll scratch yours' and it has worked throughout history. If the area of knowledge mobilisation is viewed as relevant to all involved – otherwise why are you pursuing it in the first place? – then most people want to have access to it.

What the Australian Panadol team wanted was to learn from other countries. Even if what they learned was not of direct use, they could at least benchmark themselves.

A further example of this was seen in a large UK financial services group, when a new set of marketing processes, tools and outputs were being compiled for use by the business in the following year. There were several brand teams who wanted to contribute their knowledge and experience in preparing marketing plans because they felt this would give them an opportunity to get started on the new process a year ahead of their colleagues.

Internal PR

Sharing what you know is a great way to get yourself noticed
Another truth is that in large organisations, sharing what you know is a way to boost your reputation as an individual, team, function or country. It's a tool to get yourself noticed and we have seen many careers that have soared because someone had the insight to use a knowledge mobilisation project as a vehicle to communicate

their knowledge and expertise. Naming contributors – giving details of who, what and where – will help. We have yet to find someone who preferred to keep their positive experiences secret in case their colleagues discovered their hidden glory.

This is also true for service and professional sectors such as banking, media and consulting. Broadcasting your success and building your reputation are musts in your career. There can be stumbling blocks, however, where the knowledge sought is about mistakes or pitfalls. Boeing was eventually successful in overcoming resistance to sharing things that went wrong during the building of its Boeing-777 aircraft, but it took painful pressure to induce its scientists and engineers to talk openly about errors and areas of ignorance as it was counter-cultural. The moral is to keep pushing; when the first few people agree, many others will follow.

The other stumbling block is in industries where success appears to be linked to maintaining a separate and superior body of knowledge to that of your colleagues. This is particularly true when there is an internal competitive environment over billings. The law is an example. What is my incentive to share what I know when it will help my colleagues (who after all are not as capable as me anyhow) to improve their performance, leaving me without my competitive advantage? There are two ways round this. One is to 'push' for change by, for example, insisting, as management consultancy McKinsey does, that project knowledge must be entered into a knowledge database before a billing code for your project will be authorised. The other is to 'pull' by starting actively to change the internal competitive culture into one of collaboration.

Being 'Nice'

Having talked about the more strategic aspects of human motivation, it's important to recognise that in most reasonable, well-run businesses, people will be motivated to share knowledge simply because they like being helpful; they like being 'nice'. This does not appear to be a culture-specific trait because we have seen examples in all places and cultures. If you ask someone to contribute some element of what they know to a knowledge mobilisation initiative, mostly they will say yes. Again, they want to see other elements in place – relevance and clarity of outcomes for instance – but given these, they will happily contribute.

> *Pre-Industrial Revolution skilled workers were expected to train up apprentices*

A related example of this is at Chrysler where the best (and usually older) mechanics and engineers contribute to what are called 'Engineering Books of Knowledge'. This is not just being nice but is an internal manifestation of the old teaching the young. It evokes the pre-Industrial Revolution system of apprenticeship where the onus was on the skilled person to train the apprentice.

But Only If I Trust You

The three ingredients mentioned above exist within one over-arching requirement which is that of trust. By this, I mean that sharing knowledge demands trust from the company as well as the participating individuals. For instance, if the company uses the knowledge to then make people redundant, or if Human Resources starts using the knowledge as a way of achieving other ends, then the knowledge sharing will dry up at both the input and output ends.

It is not enough to believe that trust is present. It must be seen to be happening at the top and across the business. Part of this is that everyone who should contribute is contributing. There should be no sense of injustice that the Japanese teams are contributing but the Germans are not; there should not be just one way knowledge traffic.

> *Lack of trust in senior management will obstruct knowledge mobilisation*

A lack of trust in the motives of senior management, based on past experience, can prevent any knowledge mobilisation taking place in any form. This was the case in a large brewing company where the staff were so nervous about how any contributions to the knowledge initiative might be used by senior management that is was impossible to gather knowledge. The place to start in such cases is on two levels. Trust needs to be established at a cultural level in the business in tandem within a tightly defined area of knowledge mobilisation in a part of the organisation that feels secure in itself. In the brewing company this meant that the distilling side of the business could pioneer knowledge mobilisation ahead of the other parts of the business.

How To Get People To Use The Knowledge

Most literature on knowledge management has focused on the issues around getting people to contribute knowledge, and for good reason. There are obstacles that need to be overcome. However, the mirror issue of getting people to access, understand and apply the knowledge is often passed over. People will naturally use the knowledge so long as it is relevant to them, won't they?

In my view, this misses a crucial element – as anyone in the communication field will endorse. You may well gather great content, real-time and highly relevant, but unless it is organised, edited, structured and communicated in as easy-to-use a form as possible, it will either not be applied at all or applied only partially. The fact is that busy people in organisations need to have knowledge presented in a way that 'demands' that they apply it.

> *Knowledge must be organised and structured so that it is easy*
> *to use*

For example, many organisations are casually developing intranets and accompanying websites, with little thought about the real needs of the people who are expected to contribute to them or how they will apply the knowledge that they hold. The belief is that simply installing an intranet and dumping a range of previously printed materials on to the sites in a hypertext format will miraculously result in powerful levels of usage.

The same process occurred in a precursor to the intranet – Lotus Notes. Popular and well-applied printed materials were installed on to the Lotus Notes groupware system. In the main, this produced poor levels of usage because the medium was poorly suited to reading and understanding, though it was good as a reference and visual system.

The content of intranets must always be superb, and superb in the context of that medium. People will not use an intranet to read long texts or learn, so don't expect a printed handbook of selling skills to work in that environment. The place to start is by understanding the capabilities of the various internal media available and using them appropriately. Some knowledge requires face-to-face contact, some needs to be in print, some electronic – but it must all be gathered, edited and communicated with the rigorous dedication that you would apply if you were expecting users in the company to pay for it out of their own pocket. See yourself as a magazine editor in a competitive marketplace, fighting with others for readers.

At TEG we have developed a communication approach to knowledge mobilisation projects that addresses the issue of effectiveness head-on. Knowledge mobilisation is carried out from beginning to end with the people who will participate in the initiative. They act as a touchstone throughout what often will be a project lasting 6–12 months.

	RESEARCH	DEVELOP	TEST	REFINE	TEST	PRODUCE	
WE WANT TO CHANGE	Research the organisation, the audience, the required change(s) and potential benefits etc.	Develop a draft approach and communication concepts, tools and techniques	Obtain feedback from the audience and the owners of the change(s)	Finalise the approach and develop final communication tools and techniques	Obtain feedback from the audience	Agree changes manage production of all materials and advise on any leaders training	THE CHANGES ARE HAPPENING

The main steps to follow

Having identified the area of knowledge to be mobilised with senior management, we then research all contributors in that field, gathering what they know and discussing possible communication media and approaches. Questions typically include:

- Do you need to get the knowledge in a visual form?
- What would you do with the knowledge practically?
- Who else would you share it with?
- How easily could it be out of date?
- How much do you need to know?
- What media do you use/like?

The answers will help us in the development of prototype media and content, to then test with sample groups of people around the business. At this point, we may sometimes have to amend recommended delivery systems if the systems the users need are different from those suggested by senior management. For example, it may be necessary to share artwork and video as part of the knowledge and many intranets cannot cope with this content nearly as well as CD ROM. Or there may be a demand for workshops to start the knowledge initiative and form personal contacts, rather than begin the initiative through a website launch.

This process of continual testing and refinement produces success, because when the knowledge mobilisation project goes 'live' it is as well produced as possible in the eyes of the users — both contributors and recipients. Having established that foundation of user-ease in content and delivery, the maintenance of a high standard is far easier. Projects that are less carefully developed quickly fall into disuse for reasons that sound quite trivial, such as: 'I couldn't see everything on one page . . . The material was always out of date . . . It was so slow to use . . . None of the content was relevant to me.'

What About Knowledge Theft?

Another area of justifiable concern for organisations (and one often voiced by active participants) is the issue of 'knowledge theft'. If we gather all this knowledge together how can we stop a competitor getting hold of it, particularly by one of our people taking some or all of it with them when they leave and join a competitor?

In my experience this is a perfectly understandable fear and the truth is that most of the time theft (or however we would describe that taking of knowledge by employees on leaving) does take place at some points. In a way, it would appear that the gathering of the knowledge induces people to take the knowledge because it seems so portable. Load it on to your laptop or put it in your briefcase and off you go.

To counteract this, organisations need to state their policy clearly and visibly on these matters, in such a way that staff are totally clear that this is a similar offence to the company as fraud or stealing money. The knowledge needs to be clearly labelled in all media as being in the copyright ownership of the company, and its removal from the company will be dealt with by legal means. This tough stance has two good effects: it will reduce the rate of knowledge theft, since the message will frighten many people, and it will deter competitors from using the knowledge because of the realisation that there could be legal consequences. Also, the competitor may not look so favourably on the new member of staff who arrives with the valuable knowledge if it is clear that the new member of staff is breaking the law.

Having said that, in my experience, knowledge that is taken is seldom really useful to competitors. Usually it is a little out of date, not easily adaptable to another organisation and lacks the tacit knowledge that it carries in the host company. Also if company A has pioneered some knowledge work, then by the time company B has caught up, company A is on to a new phase of knowledge work.

Is It All About Technology? No, It's Content That Counts

Mobilising knowledge is important – how do you meet the challenge? As said earlier in this chapter, companies are increasingly looking to sophisticated technology to solve the problem. Certainly technology is a key enabler; this situation, however, is akin to the advent of the telephone. We have the hardware (the telephone itself) and the software (the contents of the conversations that take place using the telephone). Having a telephone does not create communication; it just enables it to take place.

Technology is a key enabler

As can be seen from the case studies in Chapter 11, technology has enabled knowledge mobilisation to become part of the corporate agenda for ever-increasing numbers of business leaders. However *technology is not the answer itself* – it is the means required to reach the answer. The key to making a difference to how knowledge is captured, shared and applied in organisations is the 'soft' stuff not the 'hard' stuff. It is the content that counts, not the technology that is used. Lotus Notes is a fine piece of software but what counts is the quality of what is on the database, the numbers of people contributing, their geographical spread, the number of times they keep the knowledge up-to-date. These issues are nothing to do with the database itself but with the quality of the knowledge put into it.

We have all had the experience of flipping through a reference book such as a dictionary or encyclopaedia and discovering that the first two words or topics you search for are not listed. We still know that a dictionary or encyclopaedia is a great medium for knowledge sharing but the quality of the ones we are using in these instances is poor. If we put too much attention on the technology and not enough on the content stored or being routed through the technology, then people in the company will quickly lose faith in your efforts at knowledge mobilisation.

The communication system in Chapter 4 was developed to mobilise knowledge about how to create medical endorsement for a brand. Initially there was no new technology used; a printed catalogue was developed (very much 'old' technology), but that didn't matter at all to the brand teams in more than 80 different countries. All they were interested in was what they would learn that was new and useful when they opened the catalogue. It was the quality of the content that counted. You can put poor content in every intranet, Lotus Notes database, Local Area Network, CD ROM etc, but it will get you nowhere.

6.
So Where Does Technology Fit In

Current solutions usually involve 'groupware' and internets that allows workers to access the same information simultaneously. For example, Silicon Graphics, the US computer company, has an internal website known as 'Silicon Junction' which carries information covering everything from engineering projects to on-line training. Every day, about half the employees call up the site. 'It has quickly become the preferred method of disseminating and accessing information company-wide,' says Ed McCracken, the Chief Executive Officer.

Andersen Consulting exchanges information throughout its business using the 'Knowledge Xchange'. This system is based on a groupware product at the heart of many knowledge mobilisation initiatives. At the end of every consultancy project, all relevant information, such as that concerning proposals, presentations, contacts etc, is loaded on to the system. Anyone who then needs to research the subject is able to download relevant information with the help of proprietary search mechanisms, known as a 'knowledge map'.

But 'tacit' knowledge is hard to capture

The system works well but has limitations. Inevitably, there are strict access controls since much of the information is confidential. Moreover, there are many sorts of expertise that cannot be written down. 'Lots of the business relies on tacit knowledge. It is very hard to capture that,' says Marcus Speh, former Director of Knowledge Management for Andersen Consulting and now Knowledge Director for Shell, the multi-national petroleum company. 'The system requires a high degree of co-operation and commitment from staff. The goal is to make professionals responsible for the development of knowledge. For the most part, people welcome the opportunity it presents. It is very much in the interests of individuals to learn quickly.'

Let's start with the obvious. Mobilising knowledge is an activity that you cannot do alone – obviously you do not need to share knowledge with yourself – but there needs to be a means to communicate for this to happen. When two people work together in an office they talk, overhear telephone conversations and share correspondence. However, if we go beyond this, say with five people working in different offices, or who spend lots of time out of the office, the communication channels need to change and technology is required to maintain the link.

Any organisation must answer the need to capture, process, structure, store, and provide access to the information needed for the company to perform in the most competitive way. Paper has traditionally been at the centre of many organisations but, today, computers, databases and communication networks are taking its place.

Consider the cost of mobilising and transmitting information *along* the hierarchical lines of an organisation. In large organisations, it is difficult and costly to ensure that all employees have a common understanding of the company's competitive positioning. It is even more difficult and costly to transmit such an understanding throughout the organisation if competitive pressures force the company to modify the positioning.

Transmitting information *up* through a hierarchy is also costly. Transactional and local information generated at the lower levels are needed for decision-making at higher levels. In the past, companies designed structures whereby information gathered at lower levels was summarised before being transmitted upwards; this meant potentially relevant details could be left out. However, today's technologies allow us to view the whole organisation as if it were on a single level; information can be made available to each individual at the level of detail needed.

Consider an organisation, such as a bank, that has many branches covering a large geographical area. In the past, credit decisions were made at a central unit where the experts would analyse the risks associated with a client's applications. All documents had to be forwarded to that unit, causing delays in the decision-making process. Today, however, technologies such as electronic mail and video-conferencing can be used to decentralise some of these decisions. Branch managers can get advice on the spot, either through computer-based applications or from an expert. Companies have reached the point where communications from the chief executive can be effectively implemented at speed using advanced communications systems.

Let's look at two examples of how IT has been used to promote knowledge mobilisation. Mrs Fields' Cookies, the US cookie chain that owns and operates more than 700 small stores, achieved profitability of more than 20 per cent of sales, year after year, for many years. How? It succeeded in achieving a uniformity of products and processes throughout the company. All decisions in all stores were made the same way, leading to the same product quality, regardless of the location of the store.

This uniformity was not obtained using layers of supervising managers – Mrs Fields' Cookies has the lowest staff-to-store ratio in the whole industry. Knowing what, when and how much to bake, or deciding whether to run a 'sidewalk promotion' are day-to-day decisions which, when well made, can transform a small store into a profitable business. Mrs Fields' Cookies needed to run the stores profitably without incurring huge personnel costs, so the company decided to use IT to help the store managers with their planning. A computer programme forecasts sales and makes baking decisions; it can even evaluate customer-service personnel. Company-wide statistics are collected every day so that customer behaviour can be predicted for different days of the week, weather conditions and location.

The store manager has voice and e-mail that allows daily, two-way contact with headquarters and the IT system supports them very effectively. He or she is usually a young person who stays with the company, on average, sixteen months. IT has enabled a company that operates with more than 100 per cent personnel turnover to have the same organisational culture in every store.

Oticon is a Danish company that designs, manufactures and sells hearing aids. Most projects involve personnel with different capabilities coming from different functional areas. In order to promote such a team-based approach, the company has organised a 'paperless' environment.

Any document that arrives at Oticon is scanned and stored in a computer. The hard copy is physically destroyed unless it has to be kept for legal reasons. All information is accessible to any authorised employee from any workstation in the company. When a new team is created, its members can move easily from one location to another, talking all their 'papers' with them. This system means that the project-based organisation is feasible to its full extent. Project-based organisations existed before the advent of computers, but the possibility of moving from one location to another with no constraints makes this type of organisation much more efficient and much easier to put into practice.

As these two examples show, IT enables organisational forms that would have been almost impossible some years ago. As new competitive challenges force organisations to be more creative with their organisational structures, IT will make their implementation possible.

So Where Does 'Lotus Notes' Fit?

Lotus Notes is a tool that is sometimes used by people and organisations to address the issue of mobilising knowledge within and beyond their immediate corporate boundaries. It was heralded as a breakthrough software product, so much so that IBM paid a staggering $3.5 billion to Lotus for its exclusive rights. It is worth taking a little time to understand why Notes has been such a resounding success.

The demand by companies everywhere to collect, analyse, organise and disseminate a wealth of business information at speed has been dramatic. Companies are accustomed to having systems to perform certain business transactions such as pay-roll and accounting, and most have made extensive use of personal computers to assist with individual tasks; however, until recently, there has been little technology available to enable the efficient and effective *sharing* of a vast array of business information across organisations. Notes has been viewed as a pioneering product because it provides a means for managing the diverse flow of information within and between organisations. This information is stored in people's heads, on their desks and in their personal computers and, as such, is difficult for others to find and access.

In the simplest cases we could be talking about a report or presentation that many people would find useful. Andersen Consulting's Knowledge Xchange allows the seamless transfer of such knowledge across the globe from one expert to another without the user and the creator knowing each other personally. In more complex cases, it could mean building a collective wisdom about certain customers that can be shared and kept current by sales people around the world.

Above all, Notes is a flexible tool that allows organisations to tailor knowledge to their own requirements and needs. As well as linking people together across geographic boundaries, Notes allows teams of workers to design and build their own tailored applications.

Users are the best people to decide what information to collect and share

The simple fact that *users* decide what information to collect and share, how to view and present it, goes a long way to explaining why Notes has gained such popularity with business people. Additionally, its success has stemmed from the speed with which applications can be developed; not in months and years, but often in days and weeks. This factor has contributed to the high return on investment that many users have reported.

In its simplest form, Notes provides the following functions:

- electronic mail, including a variety of attachments
- computer-mediated conferencing (discussion databases)
- shared databases created through 'forms' and accessed via 'views'
- applications development through the databases which can be mail-enabled
- basic workflow automation through this environment
- databases and mail can be held on separate servers; these are updated by a process called replication
- laptop users can also exchange updates through modem-based exchange (replication) with a server

Lotus Notes has probably taken off in a way that its creator, Ray Ozzie, could scarcely have imagined. Even the almighty Bill Gates of Microsoft has had to accept the power of Notes, saying in May 1990: 'Let's face it. Notes is a great piece of software . . . one of the most exciting Windows applications you can find today.'

But What About The Intranet Isn't That It?

Many believe that internal company 'internets' – intranets – are the real future. They will easily integrate with existing Lotus Notes, the internet and world wide web. BT, the UK telecommunications company, and AT&T, the US telecommunications company, are two large organisations that early on built corporate intranets as the basis of their organisation information requirements. How they integrate them in their new joint venture remains to be seen.

Intranets should allow a direct and immediate response

It is worth saying that intranets will have to be improved dramatically if they are to provide long-term benefits. For many companies, a combination of the internet (with fire walls) and CD ROM can still provide a better communication solution than a slow and ponderous intranet.

For Charles Lowe of BT, the rationale for building BT's intranet was the increasing globalisation of its business which had resulted in problems with:

- slow paper transmission
- access and storage
- the accelerating pace of business – and thus information having to go further, faster and to more people than ever before. At BT, this was not solved by providing e-mail to 60,000 users.

Now, post-intranet, information is more timely, relevant and easy to find. The intranet has completely changed the way that people at BT are doing business. It has become BT's 'central nervous system', reacting and responding in real-time. It:

- allows employees to focus on important issues – no junk
- forces a rapid response from users
- provides real-time feedback to adjust actions
- provides global reach
- has no delaying relays
- allows a more efficient use of resources
- provides savings in time and paper – communication is

faster and more efficient
- provides an important link for virtual workgroups
- allows top-down communication – senior management is in direct contact with business users. A characteristic of a central nervous system is the concept of a direct and immediate response; it allows ready access to directors and managers.

A global, corporate intranet has allowed people at BT to 'See it, Track it, Access it', and has resulted in improved communication and better morale. Business change is the key to reaping benefits from such an investment and therefore ownership issues are important. Technologies may include:

- groupware
- internet
- intranet – 'deployment and use of internet/web technologies *within* an organisation'
- extranet – 'deployment and use of internet/web technologies *between* one organisation and another'

7.
Who Should Be Involved In Knowledge Mobilisation?

In the early 1990s, a multi-national car manufacturer held a knowledge sharing seminar. Thirty or so plant managers, drawn from ten different countries, were asked to chart the relationships they had in the company. The initial question was simple: 'Which people do you have contact with elsewhere in the company and where are they located?'

A 'map' of the organisation and its sites was placed on a wall and, for thirty minutes or so, the managers used coloured pens to mark their relationships. Then, they all stood back and surveyed their network. It was immediately obvious that there were large swathes of the company that were uncharted territory for anyone in the room – whole parts of the business with which no one had any working relationship. Conversely, there were certain links between sites that were extremely well-ploughed by many managers.

People share knowledge with people they know personally
However, the most powerful lesson learned from the chart was

that the relationships people had (and the knowledge that was shared through those relationships) were with individuals whom managers had actually met face-to-face. It seems obvious, but is worth stating none the less, that people share knowledge with other people they have met or know personally. All communication technologies, magazines, videos or phone directories have little impact on the reality that knowledge mobilisation at its most effective comes from people meeting (and forming a bond of some sort) with other people.

The group of managers also realised that it was at coffee breaks or the like, that this informal relationship-building took place. They decided to institute more frequent coffee breaks at corporate gatherings like this one, to promote the opportunities for meeting new contacts. The idea of extending the length of the coffee break was rejected as the intensity that comes from only having 15 minutes to drink and meet was reduced if more time was available. It was also thought possible that the relationships formed at such gatherings could be more valuable to the company, in the longer term, than the content of the gathering itself. Many companies would agree with that sentiment. Perhaps company gatherings should really be viewed as a range of *ad hoc* coffee breaks, interrupted by speeches from the senior management on next year's priorities.

It's All About People Talking

Always remember that knowledge mobilisation strategies, infra-structures and models will only work if the goal is to have people with knowledge meet other people with knowledge and form relationships through which their knowledge can be shared.

The approaches set out by large successful Japanese companies in the past thirty years are highly illuminating in this area. The attitude to knowledge sharing in the likes of Canon, Honda, Sharp and Matsushita has been (and to a large extent still is) starkly different to that of Western companies. It is also important to note that the culture of these companies is fundamentally different to similar-sized Western companies. The individual working for a Japanese company has a much closer identification with the company as a whole than occurs in highly individualised Western companies. Lessons can be learned, but what works in Honda will not work directly in AT&T.

Individuals help the organisation grow

In Western organisations, the approach to knowledge mobilisation has been highly structured and mechanistic – hence the emphasis is on 'managing' knowledge, introducing knowledge-transfer processes and systems. The Japanese approach tends to be what we might describe as holistic and extremely loose. In the West, we tend to link together independent individuals, while the Japanese tend to see one organism where the individuals are not independent but act as a lubricant, helping the organisation grow and run smoothly.

In his ground-breaking article, 'The Knowledge-Creating Company', Ikujiro Nonaka illustrated how personal (and selfless) knowledge sharing can be, and the drama of its impact. In the mid-eighties, product developers from the Matsushita Electric Company were hard at work on a new home bread-making machine for the local market. Their main difficulty was getting the machine to knead the dough properly. They studied the problem thoroughly, even comparing X-rays of dough kneaded by machine and by professional bakers, but without success.

Identify 'hidden' knowledge and turn it into action

Then, a software developer proposed a creative solution. The Osaka International Hotel had a reputation for making the most wonderful bread in the city – what about modelling that? The software developer spent a year training with the hotel's head baker and testing ideas on Matsushita's prototype bread-maker. He saw that the baker had a distinctive way of stretching the dough so special ribs were added to the machine to reflect the baker's technique. In its first year of sales, the new machine achieved record sales for a new piece of kitchen equipment. The software developer turned the tacit knowledge of the head baker into a form of explicit engineering knowledge that could be shared easily.

One of the roles of a Japanese manager is to identify the tacit or hidden knowledge at the front-line of the business and turn it into an actionable piece of explicit or overt knowledge. As seen from the communication system story in Chapter 4, the global marketing manager, identified an area of hidden knowledge in the business – how to develop a medical heritage for a brand. Through gathering and sharing that hidden knowledge, he made it public currency.

This same ability can be found when we look at the Japanese Quality Circles, so evident in the automobile industry in the seventies and eighties. The manufacturing teams share knowledge amongst themselves and often action it without the involvement of anyone other than their supervisor. Where improvements are found that are beyond the team's remit to implement, they move upwards via the supervisor. This is a movement from tacit to explicit knowledge through people and structure.

Well-run customer service businesses share knowledge on a daily basis

All well-run customer service businesses require such daily knowledge sharing to take place, usually with a focus on quality improvements for the customer. In the UK, the pioneering and extremely successful Prêt-à-Manager high-street sandwich chain has maintained an obsessive reputation for the quality of its food and service. This is achieved in part through daily knowledge sharing between staff before the shop opens, and by a culture of communication and improvement throughout the day, driven by the manager in charge. At levels above the front-line staff, managers of the chain are continually seeking and actioning ideas (or knowledge) from customers and staff on how to improve quality. It is worth noticing that this privately owned and still fairly small business has more in common culturally with Matsushita than it does with British Telecom.

Finding Out Where Knowledge Lives

Develop a 'Knowledge Map' to guide you to your destination
You need a map to get to any destination – unless you have been to the place before. The information can come directly from a map, from someone else who has a map or someone who has it 'in their head'. Likewise, if you need someone's knowledge about something, you have to know where to look. One way to help people find what they need to know is to develop a 'knowledge map'. This could be printed, stored on a central database or whatever. Like a phone book, it guides you to the destination but doesn't tell you in detail what you will find when you get there.

The map is a picture of what the company knows and can be updated to show how that store of knowledge is developing or (after a downsizing or a merger) shrinking. The organisation chart is better than nothing but not much better. Your personal network can help you find the source, but it is easier if the gathering is done by an impartial researcher.

Microsoft created a people-orientated knowledge map: the information systems group decided to map the knowledge of systems developers with the aim of linking people to jobs and workteams. Once the IT people have a clearer idea of what knowledge is needed by the people using the map, then they will contribute to the proposed project more effectively.

Each person is evaluated for competence, with increasing levels of competence recorded at different career points; from found-ation level when they join Microsoft, to local competence, then advanced skills to global knowledge. Within each of the four levels there are two categories – explicit knowledge (covering Excel or other software) and implicit (such as abstract thinking). There are nearly 400 implicit and explicit competences in the company. Another 'cut' for each competency is the skill level of the person from basic to expert, which is described in a few lines in a measurable way.

A complex profile is put together for new assignments. Usually, it specifies about fifty competences that are needed and at what levels. The manager compiling the project can then ask the on-line system for the top ten candidates who meet the profile and the database provides the names. Obviously, this type of mapping can be done for any area that the company views as extremely valuable. However, it is a time-consuming process to compile and maintain up-to-date information and so the map must be used to support the overall business strategy.

8.

Using Internal Communication To Bring Knowledge Mobilisation To Life

Involving People Is At The Heart Of Great Knowledge Mobilisation

We are experiencing an unprecedented period of development in internal communication. Communication is at the heart of making any business change happen; knowledge mobilisation is no exception. So how should organisations involve people so that they can become knowledge mobilisers? Let's start with a story.

Over dinner, with twenty managers from an electronics multinational, I witnessed a conversation between two of them. One Russian said passionately: 'It's not even that it has made my life easier, it's the heart of how I work.' A Dutch manager agreed: 'For us it's the way we run our business.' They were discussing a long-running initiative to improve the marketing processes of their company. It covers a broad spread of areas such as advertising development, market research and brand planning. The remarkable thing about this exchange is not that two culturally different managers could share similar working experiences, but that both could hold such strong, even emotional, beliefs about something as often unwelcome as yet another organisational change programme.

So, why would two managers feel so intensely about a drive to introduce better working approaches across a multi-national? Not simply because the change programme used terrific media, content and workshops, but because more than 1,000 people felt powerful levels of ownership, commitment and attachment to their new processes. Why? Because they created them.

Achieving 'ownership' has already happened
Since 1994, nearly 200 managers (one-fifth of the company's marketing population) have been involved in developing each annual wave of modules in what has become a regular cycle of

You have to get people involved to get real ownership of Knowledge Mobilisation involvement and joint development. By the time the new modules are launched, 20 per cent of managers have already shared in the development. Achieving 'ownership' is not a problem; it's already happened.

This is just one example of how approaches to bringing organisational change to life have moved ahead in the nineties; in leading companies, this has often happened at a frantic pace. The days when introducing corporate change meant well-fashioned efforts to achieve 'employee buy-in' are long gone. We are now in an era when nothing less than absolute ownership of change and new levels of employee involvement are required. Joint development of change initiatives now lies with the people who will make the change live or die.

Take the case of Levis. In the past eight years, it has faced a need to re-shape the company to meet challenges from new and faster entrants into its markets and it began a company-wide change without a polished strategy for success. To begin with, it cleared an entire floor of its headquarters building and brought together more than 100 people drawn from across its businesses. Their task was to transform Levis. They owned the change because their efforts created it and their involvement produced similar levels of participation amongst their colleagues.

If I 'buy-in', then I can also 'buy-out'

Most major organisational change initiatives fail because of a lack of 'buy-in'. 'Internal marketing' – applying external marketing techniques to employees – was a step forward, but far more potent involvement and ownership approaches are now being used with powerful bottom line results. The problem with striving for buy-in is that if I 'buy-in' to the change (be it a new process, customer service, new structure etc), then I can subsequently 'buy-out'. On the other hand, as both stories demonstrate, if I am involved directly in creating and developing the change, then I cannot help but make it work because it is mine.

As can be seen from the table on the following page, there has been a gradual (and, more recently, an accelerated) shift along a scale of employee involvement and ownership. Such tables simplify the picture but, broadly speaking, in the fifties, sixties and seventies, there was the phase of 'tell', when management told you what was happening, followed by the time of 'sell', when management 'sold' benefits to people.

COMMUNICATION METHOD	TELL	SELL	"BUY-IN"	CONSULT	CO-DEVELOP
MESSAGE	YOU WILL!!!	THIS WILL BE REALLY GOOD!	LOOK WHAT YOU'LL GET OUT OF THIS	WHAT DO YOU REALLY NEED?	WHAT SHOULD WE BUILD TOGETHER?
LEVEL OF OWNERSHIP	VERY LOW	LOW	AVERAGE	HIGH	VERY HIGH

More involvement = more ownership

In the eighties this gave way to 'buy-in'; companies 'marketed' change to their own people, as they did to their external consumers. If you were targeted, you would buy the change. Leading organisations are now, as a minimum, consulting their people when change is required. Many are exploring the exciting and rewarding phase of joint creation, where the change is embedded into people's day-to-day life through a process of joint development. The fact is we are passionate about the things that we hold dear – things we create and own. What once seemed adventurous communication approaches are no longer enough for people to bring their hearts and minds to the organisations they work for. Organisations want and need genuine ownership of, and commitment to change. To achieve this, people should be seen as partners in joint creation, not as consumers to be marketed to.

We are passionate about things we create
Successful knowledge mobilisation depends on the involvement

of people in the development of how the company approaches the issue, as well as ensuring that knowledge is actually shared as an everyday business activity. The danger is that a knowledge mobilisation initiative could be driven by a narrow team who fail to involve the people who would make the initiative succeed. Any knowledge mobilisation project should be co-developed with a sample of the people who will be making the project happen when it goes 'live'.

Involve The People Who Will Make It Happen

In 1993, British Petroleum Exploration, the part of the UK oil giant that discovers and extracts oil and gas, decided to restructure itself into forty-two independent business centres. These business centres would have the freedom to develop processes and solutions that fitted their own needs. John Browne, the Managing Director of BP, thought that the best local ideas could be applied in the larger business. It was an attempt to hold on to the benefits of a small business as well as those of a large corporation.

For this to happen, a superb system for communicating and sharing between the forty-two centres was needed. A pilot, known as the Virtual Teamwork Programme, was developed to enable centres to work independently but also collaborate quickly and easily. The objective was to let the people with knowledge talk easily when they needed to, rather than document their knowledge. It was decided that the team driving this project would be drawn from the different centres, rather than from IT, despite the heavy IT input into the project (they had provided, installed and trained people to use desktop video-conferencing, e-mail, multimedia, scanners, groupware and web browser).

A Change Management team was added to the project to help train the participants in the range of technologies used. This involvement of users throughout the development (and the idea of piloting the entire project to get feedback from users) led to a project that was based around people being able to create their own networks and share resources, materials and visual items. If the IT people had driven the venture, the technology would no doubt have worked well but it would not have been used to full effect.

The virtual teamwork project's success was proved by the volume of use by keen participants and the savings in time and money. On one occasion, an equipment shut-down brought operations to a standstill on a North Sea mobile drilling ship. The drilling engineers placed a video camera in front of the faulty piece of equipment and connected it to one of the BP Virtual Teamwork stations. They talked to an expert in Aberdeen, via satellite, who examined the piece of equipment, made suggestions and achieved the repairs. The overall cost saving using this system was around £100,000 and the shut-down lasted a few hours rather than a full day.

A Knowledge Culture – Your Most Powerful Ally

Culture is the issue on which knowledge mobilisation can stand or fall.

It is fair to say that in most writing on knowledge mobilisation, the role of culture is covered as one of a number of issues critical for success. However, as can be seen from the Japanese organisations in Chapter 7, culture is the most fundamental ingredient. If your culture supports, encourages and rewards knowledge sharing, as at 3M, SmithKline Beecham or Nokia, then other ways of promoting knowledge mobilisation will fall on fertile ground. However, if there is a basic mistrust of knowledge sharing then, despite the new technologies, targets and reporting lines, the initiative will fail.

One global financial services firm discovered this painful fact for themselves: restructuring the business with new jobs and new titles did little to change the way the company worked on a daily basis and, most importantly, how it approached its customers. The cultural issues that were obstructing progress had not been addressed at all, a difficulty since the process of changing how people behaved had to come before the structure changes could work.

A similar story comes from another financial services firm which developed a powerful programme of customer service and quality improvement which failed to deliver its planned benefits because the levels of trust within the company were so low. People believed that the programme was a 'plot' by senior management to meet a hidden agenda. If you believe that your organisation is likely to find the idea of knowledge mobilisation threatening or challenging to its norms, then the place to start (before any knowledge mobilisation work gets under way) is with the culture.

Culture change can be achieved in many different ways depending on the nature of the company or people involved. However, some common questions and issues need to be investigated and answered by people at all levels of the business:

- How do people get on in this business?
- What kind of performance is rewarded?
- What happens if you help others here?
- What happens if you share knowledge here?
- What experiences have you had giving or getting knowledge?
- What would need to happen for this business to change?
- What do you need to see happening and by whom?

These questions dig into the issues that every company faces. If they are not tackled before the work starts then the initiative will quickly hit an obstacle. Maybe people won't contribute, or contribute only inconsequential knowledge, and not seek out knowledge when they need it.

9.
The Twelve Steps to Knowledge Mobilisation

One of the most popular questions about knowledge mobilisation is: 'Where do I start?' If you have been reading this book from its beginning, then you probably have some ideas on that already. If, like many readers, you dip into books at different points, here is a summary of some points made earlier organised into twelve steps to mobilising knowledge in your company.

Some steps can be completed at the same time, as can been seen from the chart on the next page. The steps can be linked together in a variety of ways, but this has not been marked on the chart as the links will vary between organisations.

Overall, remember that knowledge mobilisation needs a supportive culture to flourish. This will encompass structure, commitment from the top, job security and the motivation of your employees to share knowledge. It is important to assess the level of knowledge that will be shared so that employees are not overloaded with information. This will prevent overlap and duplication, while also capturing the knowledge of your workers and empowering them by sharing expertise.

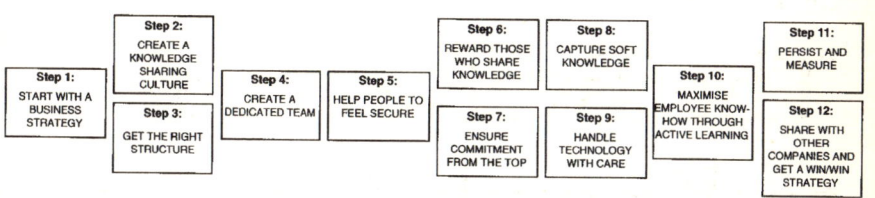

The 12 Steps to Knowledge Mobilisation

The knowledge mobilisation process should be measurable and tied to the goals of the business

The process needs to be measurable and aligned with your business goals. The art of knowledge mobilisation is in managing the process of sharing information between parts of the company in a win/win situation.

Step 1: Start With A Business Strategy

The primary purpose of a company is to provide services and products that people choose to buy instead of those of the company's competitors. Before spending time and effort changing the way you work, you must ensure you understand your business strategy to which knowledge mobilisation can contribute.

In Chapter 4 we saw how the marketing divisions of a pharmaceutical company wanted to build the medial heritage of its main brand. It approached its marketing departments to ask what knowledge they could provide to help with this task. The marketing departments wanted to know what other marketing departments were doing, but in a format that was simple and visual. From this need, a printed and electronic catalogue was born. The catalogue included successful examples of advertising, public relations and sales promotion campaigns from around the world.

Each example was presented in a standard format; relevant information included the market background, their idea, the results, a contact name for that department, as well as visuals of the example. The catalogue has allowed cross-fertilisation of ideas between markets, necessary in building their global brand.

Knowledge sharing initiatives can help to regulate the flow of information

Many knowledge sharing initiatives also help to regulate the flow of information. Companies are increasingly aware of the danger in overloading their employees with information. It is interesting to note that, when originally assessing their role in interviewing employees, Ernst & Young's knowledge team saw gaps in information management as well. Employees did not know where to get information; they saw the proposed initiative as the first step to organising the company's knowledge.

During the recent merger with Sun Alliance and the consequential restructuring, Royal Insurance found that it was necessary to keep its communication tightly focused. At the end of the day, employees wanted to know: 'How will this affect me?', 'What's my job going to be?' and, 'Who will I report to?' The company opened an electronic bulletin board and invited people to send in their questions for management to post their responses. All employees had access to the board, so this method prevented repetitive questions.

Technology has had a positive impact in determining what is useful to employees. It enables employees to seek information themselves as they need it. The intranet's greatest asset is that it uses a 'pull' rather than a 'push' system; this encourages people while allowing them to move at their own pace.

Step 2: Create A Knowledge-Sharing Culture

Creating a knowledge-sharing culture can take many years, but every step takes you closer. Ernst & Young realised that it had cultural obstacles to overcome in order to encourage knowledge sharing. It recognised the paradox between the traditional culture of client confidentiality and its goal of encouraging its employees to share what they have learnt from cases. In actual fact, employees are not breaking client confidentiality by sharing information between colleagues; Ernst & Young had to overcome this perception barrier to create knowledge sharing.

> *Employees are not breaking client confidentiality by sharing information*

Remploy, the company which specialises in the hiring of disabled staff, has introduced critical paths which aim to make its employees more proactive in their knowledge sharing. The company ensures that every employee is aware of everyone else's role around them, so they can turn to the right person when seeking knowledge. This has empowered employees by allowing them to take responsibility for finding the knowledge they need in speaking to the right people.

Other companies have created centralised databases for and about their employees. Allowing people to understand who is the expert on what encourages employees to turn to each other for information and knowledge. Digital Equipment Corporation Professional Services Organisation maintains a database of its consultants' profiles. Resourcing for a consulting contract is made easier through matching the consultant's skills and expertise with the requirements for the task.

Tackling a culture that says 'knowledge is power' is a huge task. If the pay and benefits systems reward the hoarding of knowledge, then these systems need to change. You cannot hide what some call the 'corporate body language' – who gets promoted and why. In this instance, promotion should come to those who share knowledge, not the reverse.

Step 3: Get The Right Structure

The structure of an organisation defines who reports to who and who works on what. Consequently, the structure will affect your knowledge mobilisation. A structure which draws different people together for projects or encourages functions to work together will naturally encourage knowledge sharing.

Flatter organisational structures encourage knowledge sharing

A flatter organisational structure encourages knowledge mobilisation. If there are too many layers within an organisation, knowledge mobilisation automatically becomes more difficult. Bureaucracies are not conducive to mobilising knowledge since the culture of 'information is power' pervades them.

The move towards mobilising knowledge has sometimes occured as part of a restructuring exercise. When SmithKline Beecham's marketing was restructured around matrix management, SB became able to take responsibility globally for brands or product categories and not be judged on a country-by-country level. The restructure automatically encourages knowledge mobilisation across the markets in each category. However, it becomes more difficult to create cross-fertilisation of ideas between different categories; this may be because they are run as separate profit centres and are therefore less likely to see the impact of mobilising knowledge on their own bottom line.

SmithKline Beecham has attempted to create more discussion between the categories and a horizontal flow of information between the networks by creating forums and meetings between the categories.

Step 4: Create A Dedicated Team

Changing the culture of an organisation is a major initiative so it needs a dedicated team to push it forward. When adopting a culture of knowledge mobilisation, it is vital to enlist support to carry it through. This can either be a dedicated group of knowledge professionals or a project team consisting of employees from various functions.

The team should:

- assess what is needed and how this fits in with achieving business goals
- review current channels of communication
- encourage and involve people in the move towards knowledge sharing
- sustain, reinforce, reward and maximise knowledge sharing

Ernst & Young realised that it had cultural obstacles to overcome in order to encourage knowledge sharing. It recognised the paradox between the traditional culture of maintaining client confidentiality and encouraging its employees to share what they have learnt from cases. In actual fact, employees are not breaking client confidentiality by sharing information with their colleagues, but this is a perception barrier that companies such as Ernst & Young had to overcome to create knowledge sharing.

A 'dedicated' team highlights the company commitment to knowledge sharing

Ernst & Young now has a large team of knowledge workers – knowledge professionals and a research team. This dedicated team is able to drive initiatives forward and monitor the results. The very existence of the team also highlights the company's commitment to knowledge sharing.

It is interesting to compare Ernst & Young with Triplex Lloyd, the engineering firm. Several Triplex Lloyd sites were facing common manufacturing problems, but failing to share problem-solving solutions. Management recruited a young engineer to be responsible for sharing the know-how between the sites. The engineer ensured that the knowledge sharing initiative was driven forward without overburdening each of the site's managing directors who had traditionally been responsible for this role. The engineer also trained employees to continue the knowledge sharing process.

Step 5: Help People To Feel Secure

Employees don't share knowledge willingly when they fear for their jobs

Employees have become wary of becoming dispensable, a concern fostered by the redundancies of the recession of the early 1990s. It is almost impossible to create an open, knowledge sharing environment when experiencing employee cut-backs. People become suspicious of each other and of management; they want to hold on to their own knowledge as a way of maintaining something unique to offer the company. Companies must be aware that employees must feel secure in their jobs in order to share their knowledge.

Sun Microsystems is undergoing tremendous growth and is having problems in recruiting to meet demand. The Director of Human Resources sees this trend as helping to create a feeling of job security for people which, in turn, enables an open approach to their work. However, a downturn in the company's fortune is also possible, so it is looking at how an open culture can be maintained. One approach it has taken is to outsource and use contract workers. It feels that this approach will help prevent forced redundancies in the future. However, it remains to be seen how much contract workers will be able to contribute to knowledge mobilisation. They usually do not feel part of the organisation; they usually feel connected to their skill area and so share knowledge among other professionals with those skills, some of whom may be in your company.

Step 6: Reward Those Who Share Knowledge

When changing a culture, you need to create methods of reinforcing the new approach to business, and remuneration is one of the most powerful ways of doing this. Respondents stressed that knowledge mobilisation contributions should be recognised in the pay structure. If employees are being rewarded for initiating methods of mobilising knowledge, or for their contribution to a team, it will assist with creating a culture where this happens.

Elizabeth Lank, Programme Director, Mobilising Knowledge at ICL, acknowledges that one of the obstacles to successfully mobilising knowledge is the WiiFM factor – 'What's in it for me?' Most reward and appraisal systems discourage information sharing if it is unrelated to immediate objectives.

At Ernst & Young and at the Boston Consulting Group, a part of each consultant's compensation depends on 'knowledge mobilisation activities'. The company hopes to dissuade individuals from viewing personal knowledge as an asset to be guarded.

Step 7: Ensure Commitment From The Top

A Culture change needs to be led by example

Commitment from the top is essential to a successful culture change. The role of the CEO is essential to culture changes. If the CEO changes, so does the company culture. SmithKline Beecham acknowledges that culture change needs to be led by example. Employees need to see top management promoting knowledge sharing if they are expected to be the same.

Sun MicroSystems uses the commitment of the CEO to reinforce its culture and motivate its employees. Regular announcements and messages from its CEO and President are delivered to employees by sending video clips via e-mail, capitalising on the technologies that every employee has on their desktop. Extensive use is made of the intranet, 'Sun Radio' broadcasts interviews with senior management on demand. These systems are integral to the open communication culture of Sun and they help to inform the 15,000 employees of any developments within the organisation.

Step 8: Capture Soft Knowledge

Connect people with people – not systems – so that the knowledge can be captured. There appears to be a correlation between how difficult knowledge is to capture and its usefulness to a company. Soft knowledge, which resides in the minds of employees, is difficult and at times impossible to access. Companies are recognising that it is vital to share ideas, creativity and opinions, as well as facts and figures, to give themselves a competitive edge.

Many companies operate systems of monitoring competitor activity. Employees are asked to contribute any information, even rumours, on their competitors through intranets and Lotus Notes databases. Each item can be discussed or added to through a feedback system; it assesses opinion rather than hard facts.

Asking employees to contribute rumours, can be an important method of keeping as up-to-date as possible with the market. In this way it is possible to prepare for potential competitor activity *prior* to its occurrence. Looking at facts along can only provide historic information.

Create multi-level networks to capture soft knowledge
One way to capture soft knowledge is to create networks so that

people can communicate with each other on more than one level. This is often very difficult to achieve in large organisations. Training programmes which bring people together can help and large companies do this for example through induction courses when trainees join the company.

Sun brings together its employees world-wide by job function (e.g. sales or technical) every year to train them in developments in both the company and the market. These meetings, which typically bring together between 1,000 and 2,500 employees, are seen as an opportunity to extend networks globally, as well as reward employees through a 'social' event.

Companies are focusing on increasing the scope for social events which encourage networking with people outside the sphere of a specific job. An example of this is the 'doughnut day' initiated by Ernst & Young. Every fortnight, people are given coffee and doughnuts and encouraged to wander around the offices, speaking to people in different departments about their jobs. This helps people to understand where they fit into an organisation and encourages them to talk to others on work-related issues.

Step 9: Handle Technology With Care

Technology can enable knowledge mobilisation, but it is useless without the necessary culture – people must want to share knowledge. The companies involved in our survey (see Chapter 10) saw that it was essential to invest in suitable channels of communication but felt that this, in itself, did little to achieve knowledge mobilisation.

Technology brings its own set of problems
Those companies that had invested heavily in technology saw it as a useful tool. However, they were aware that it also brings its own

set of problems. The Human Resource managers, in particular, were concerned that face-to-face meetings were being replaced by electronic communication. David Bacon of BAT reflected the consensus; he believes that: 'There is no replacement for eye-balling.'

However, the benefits of technology (when used properly) cannot be overlooked:

- It can create the lateral spread of information; people at the same level in an organisation will talk to each other, rather than having information passed down to them through hierarchical channels.
- It makes sharing knowledge feasible, both logistically and economically.
- It can prevent information overload by offering people a 'pull', not a 'push'.

Ogilvy and Mather, like many companies, was quick to install e-mail; they see it as an excellent tool, particularly when communicating world-wide. As we have all experienced, e-mail can also assist with horizontal channels of communication, enabling employees to contact each other directly.

However, in general, the participants in our survey felt that technology itself did not accomplish alone mobilising knowledge. E-mail was also thought to have limited potential for knowledge sharing. In comparison, groupware – such as Lotus Notes – or an intranet were thought to have great potential by creating interactive discussion groups.

The introduction of an intranet at the BBC had a radical effect throughout the corporation. Traditionally, it had been difficult to contact employees to get information out across the organisation. Employees were excited by the rapid introduction of the intranet and the prospect of having information at their fingertips. It also changed the administrative processes; for example, all studio bookings were carried out over the intranet.

Step 10: Maximise Employee Know-how Through Active Learning

Investment in employee training is rising at a rapid rate. As competitive pressures increase, companies are spending more and more on training selected employees in specialist areas; this naturally creates islands of expertise. This can be minimised by ensuring that these employees can share their new-found knowledge by cascading learning through the organisation.

Cross-functional knowledge sharing increases awareness of roles and responsibilities

Similarly, functions within large organisations are becoming increasingly distinct in their skills and operations. Using the intranet and similar systems enables cross-functional knowledge transfers, increasing awareness of functional roles and responsibilities as well as maintaining a relationship between departments.

Sun Microsystems has created an 'ambassador' programme where one person is the champion for a product in a particular geographic area. The ambassador receives information from the marketing/product development departments, and is also responsible for attending specialised training. Ambassadors also communicate with each other, exchanging thoughts and experiences with their particular products, as well as discussing formulas to defeat competitors. They then disseminate their knowledge amongst their colleagues, sharing pertinent information that will help them on a day-to-day basis. This reinforces understanding of the subject and allows others to benefit from their expertise.

Allen & Overy's junior lawyers present their experiences and areas of expertise to the new entrants; partners also give presentations at other levels. This creates a continuous process of learning from each other.

Step 11: Persist And Measure

Participants in our survey knew that when people leave the company, they take their training and know-how with them. To minimise the impact of a departing employee, companies should capture as much as possible of that person's knowledge before they leave. This could be done through continuous participation in knowledge mobilisation systems.

An exit interview is another useful way of recording an individual's history at a company. The interview should be carried out by an expert to ensure that the most useful information is extracted. Access to such interviews is an excellent starting point for the newcomer in understanding their role, the culture and some of the softer issues of their new position.

At Kraft Food, the company's oral history archive has been used to fashion a new marketing approach to an old product. Towards the end of the 1980's, one of the company's brands, Cracker Barrel cheese, was not selling well. Linda Crowder, the Brand Manager, used the archive to delve into the brand's origins in order to shape a new marketing strategy. The transcripts of the interviews provided her with the insights of the National Sales Manager of cheese products from 1958 to 1962, the period when the brand's sales began to take off. 'He gave us a perspective we just couldn't get anywhere else,' she says. 'Our research gave us a sense of what the theory was when Cracker Barrel was first introduced, and what we told consumers about the brand in the beginning.

Define criteria and introduce instruments to measure success
It is essential to define success criteria and introduce instruments to measure the impact on the business before a project is implemented. The effective implementation of a knowledge mobilisation project will be systemic to the organisation, so the measurements may have to be fairly loose and abstract.

Existing financial measurements cannot offer an adequate

measurement of a company's intellectual assets. It is unlikely that this will ever appear on a balance sheet in quantitative terms. Ernst & Young is currently assessing the situation and determining how it will measure its success. However, if it sets a goal of winning x amount of new accounts, for example, there are many other factors which will influence the outcome; knowledge mobilisation cannot be judged alone.

The knowledge mobilisation project champions can measure the success of the project by capturing and sharing the benefits that people have found from using the system. If possible, give each benefit a financial value and keep a 'total': if someone closes a sale through knowledge gained from the initiative, record its value to the business. The knowledge mobilisation initiative will either prove its worth quickly and not need measurement, or it can be left to fall into disuse.

Step 12: Share With Other Companies And Get A Win/Win Strategy

Be open to the idea of sharing non-sensitive information with other companies – it's better for this process to be managed than for you to turn a blind eye to unofficial channels of information sharing.

Information can be shared through trade organisations, strategic alliances or other networks. Great savings can be made by sharing knowledge and pooling resources with other companies. It is interesting to note that the results of our knowledge sharing report are being shared by all the participants; in itself, the report is a knowledge mobilisation exercise.

Be clear on what information can and can't be shared
British American Tobacco (BAT) works with its competitors to lobby governments. However, David Bacon, Head of Corporate Communications, knows that the line between information that

can and can't be shared is blurred; all employees must understand the implications and, if necessary, ask for guidance.

The pharmaceutical industry is moving towards working with competitors to 'manage' a disease from beginning to end. There are great cost savings to be made, especially in research and development, by developing this process. It offers a more efficient way of serving the client, whether the client is the NHS or the patient.

IBM's Normal Ashton reflects this consensus and sees most competitors as customers, partners and suppliers through the strategic alliances formed between IBM's departments with those of its competitors. Most companies do not actively share information with their competitors, although they are aware that it takes place informally through:

- job-swapping within the industry
- networks of colleagues and friends, especially within industries with high turnover of staff (such as IT)
- some non-competitive departments, such as HR, acting collectively to set standards within their industry

So What Are The Pitfalls?

Perhaps the toughest part of knowledge mobilisation – besides defining it – is finding what you need when you need it. Andersen Consulting's London office cannot benefit from a market study completed by the Sao Paulo group two years ago if the Londoners do not know where their colleagues stashed their report – or even that it exists. Organisations must create and maintain easy-to-use 'knowledge maps' or navigational tools.

Too much information is worse than none at all
Sloppy attempts at knowledge mobilisation can quickly escalate into serious information overload. Companies that simply stockpile

data with little or no organisation often find that, given strains on storage space, and time wasted looking for misplaced materials, too much information is worse than none at all. Effective knowledge mobilisation requires a supportive, collaborative culture and the elimination of traditional rivalries. For some employees, this may mean painfully 'unlearning' long-standing lessons. Someone who interprets the old axiom 'knowledge is power' as 'to stay strong, I've got to hide and protect what I know' isn't likely to embrace the concept of mobilisation resources.

Successful efforts leave no room for inconsistency, inaccessibility or isolated islands of expertise. Knowledge mobilisation becomes a parody, a source of bitter internal conflict, if resources are not equally accessible across the board, in every department and all remote locations, twenty-four hours a day.

Knowledge Does Not Live By Information Technology Alone

'Even the most user-friendly tools will not help with managing information unless they are strongly linked to people and processes,' says Thomas H. Davenport, Director of the Information Systems Management programme at the University of Texas at Austin. 'Knowledge dies when it is disembodied.' By way of example, Davenport describes an engineering and construction company's attempt to preserve its best-practice expertise. The effort failed largely because nobody edited the materials for consistency or relevance, and those who contributed information did not include their names so nobody knew where to turn with questions.

Watch Out For Duplication

Mobilising knowledge prevents the duplication of other people's work. Information on past and current work should be held centrally so that it is available to all employees. Boots plc, with over 50,000 employees, wanted to find out who was buying-in external information in its organisation. It decided to do this by constructing a company-wide information map. A questionnaire was sent out to discover what market research or literature was being bought-in and whether it was needed.

People often buy information, rather than seek it within their own organisation

According to Dr Steve Hewitt, Head of Group Information Services, the results showed duplication of purchases and hidden pockets of information, highlighting that many company workers buy information rather than share it or seek it elsewhere within the organisation. Boots implemented a process of scanning trade journals, market research and other bought-in materials to encourage all employees to use the common information/ knowledge base and to save costs.

Finally, it is tough to translate results to the bottom line. Of the eighty corporations surveyed by Andersen Consulting during a knowledge conference, more than three-quarters thought knowledge mobilisation an essential or important part of their business strategy. However, more than 90 per cent admitted that they had not yet developed reliable ways to link knowledge mobilisation to financial results. The researchers concluded that: 'While companies may be starting to measure knowledge assets, the link to financial results remains fuzzy. The lack of progress in this area, and the uncertainty of whether it is even important, could ultimately torpedo knowledge mobilisation initiatives.'

Not Sharing The Same Language

By this, I do not mean a common *spoken* language, though that is obviously an issue for some organisations. However, most global organisations expect, above a certain level, to be able to communicate in a common language, usually English.

A more common problem for multi-nationals is that technical terms are different throughout the world and not understood across the organisation. The Malaysia office uses a four-stage new product development process, while the French manager uses a seven-step process with different terms within it. How can they share knowledge if they cannot even share a common understanding of their own business?

> *Sound processes are tremendous enablers of knowledge*
> *mobilisation*

Sound global processes that are followed by everyone in all areas of the business are tremendous enablers of knowledge mobilis- ation. The terms and wording within these processes should be consistent and planning formats used can be the same. However, this does not prevent some customisation to suit local needs, as long as, at a higher level, there is a common approach and understanding. 'If I send you my Customer Promotions State- ment and you send me yours, we can compare differences relating to the global customer which the format covers.' Now there is dialogue; with this commonality there is no waste of time and no frustration.

10.
What a UK Survey On Knowledge Revealed

As part of research for this book, TEG carried out a survey into knowledge mobilisation in the UK. The objective of the survey was to look at how organisations mobilise the power of what they know and assess current knowledge sharing practices.

A questionnaire containing a request for examples of knowledge sharing was sent to 540 companies. In keeping with the subject of the project, the findings were shared with all participants.

The second stage of the research took the form of in-depth interviews with the person responsible for knowledge management in a cross-section of blue-chip companies. Those chosen were recognised as taking an active approach to knowledge management. We wanted to reflect what companies were currently doing in this area, and the issues they believe affect successful knowledge sharing.

Briefly, this is what we learnt.

The Knowledge Movement
Is Pervasive

Whether knowledge mobilisation is defined in terms of learning, intellectual capital, knowledge assets, intelligence, know-how, insight or wisdom, the conclusion is the same: manage it better or perish. Initiatives throughout industry, the education sector and government are trying to tackle the same problems, issues and opportunities.

Treat people as assets, not liabilities or expenses

The unmeasurable must be measured. Traditional financial accounting mechanisms fail to calculate the most important resources of the firm – intellectual capacity. Current mechanisms often treat people as liabilities or expenses instead of assets. The benefits must be defined in order to justify necessary investment strategies in the human and social (i.e. interactive) capital of the firm.

Implementation Takes Many Forms

New titles and initiatives vary from company to company because each corporate culture is unique. There may be totally new titles and jobs, or a re-labelling of traditional functions. There are many ways to gather knowledge, but leadership in this area can come from any level, function or position in the company.

The Nature Of 'The Community' Must Be
Understood And Harnessed

Businesses have multiple stakeholders: suppliers, partners, allies, customers and – in some cases competitors. The 'Knowledge Community' is a combination of evolving systems and people and needs carefully architected schemes for profitable growth. Focus on the definition of the 'community' and then inter-connect the pieces.

Technology Is Integral To The Successful Functioning Of The Knowledge Enterprise

There is widespread confusion as to the appropriate role for supporting technology. Technology 'eats' up a lot of knowledge budgets but a 'technology backlash' is building due to poor practical results from it.

The Knowledge Phenomenon Must Be Managed And Not Left To Chance

Knowledge management is both a science and an art
As incomplete as systems may be, some influence and control is better than none at all. Unexpected forces and events can cause a major shift in your business. Management of knowledge must therefore be practised as both a science and an art in order to maximise the advantage.

Clear Responsibility For Mobilising Knowledge Is Essential

Knowledge mobilisation encompasses information technology, internal communications, human resources and change manage-ment. Ideally, or at least initially, there should be a dedicated team to develop, drive forward and maintain initiatives. This may be a project team drawn from relevant disciplines or, as in some major consultancies, a separate, autonomous department.

What This Tells Us

Most companies are aware of the need to mobilise the power of what they know with half actively attempting to address the need. But the specifics of what they are doing can seem quite mundane in comparison with the grand nature of the topic. The theory of knowledge mobilisation sounds as if it will 'set the world on fire' but, when businesses discuss their actual practices, one business area or function is usually tackling one particular area of need that in itself can seem mundane.

Knowledge sharing does not stop at the front door; organisations see the role of knowledge sharing as valid with suppliers and customers; involve your 'extended organisation' – dealers, distributors and contracted salesforces. The example of NCR's Knowledge Lab in Chapter 11 shows the potential benefits of this approach.

11.
Case Studies

These case studies look at what 15 companies are doing about Knowledge Mobilisation. Inevitably, developments advance quickly in this area and while these case studies were up-to-date ahead of publication, by the time you read this there will be some new improvements and experiences. Contact the company directly to hear about them.

3I GROUP plc

Background

Formed in 1945, 3i has since invested over £8 billion in over 12,000 companies, and currently holds investments in around 3,200 businesses, both in the UK and internationally. The company typically makes 500-600 investments each year. More than 900 companies in which 3i has invested have subsequently been listed on a stock market.

It is the UK's leading specialist investor in unquoted companies. It makes investments in a wide range of businesses which do not have ready access to capital markets. It has a network of 18 offices in the UK and nine in continental Europe, has recently opened an office in Singapore, and has a joint venture in Japan.

Context

Networking is a crucial part of 3i's business. The formal and informal networks that exist within the company serve to match businesses with new or additional people, and buyers with sellers. Since the mid-1980s it has realised the need to manage its use of corporate knowledge, networks and memory – the historic contacts built up by 3i staff.

The technology to manage coherently this mass of internal knowledge networks was not readily available until recently. However, in the last eighteen months, 3i has rolled out its Windows-based 'Knowledgebase' (also known as 'Watson'), which contains detailed information on industry sectors and on companies that the organisation has researched. It also has MIDAS (marketing and Information Database), a bespoke database also based on Windows, which serves as an internal, company-wide filofax.

The Challenge

A team of twenty-five industry advisers operate from offices near Birmingham while the investment teams are dotted around various regional offices in the UK. Since the industry advisers spend a considerable amount of time on the road, the investment teams were often unable to contact them. To quote Rod Perry, Director of Group Services, the company needed to 'time-shift the knowledge' which existed within the organisation and make it readily available and accessible to users.

The industry advisers, who are a key link between 3i and potential clients, were able to amass a wealth of knowledge about companies all around the UK. However, the company was not in a position to use this knowledge to its advantage. In addition, changes in industry and commerce required individuals within the industry teams to specialise. This sometimes created a backlog of visit requests.

What Happened?

Knowledgebase and MIDAS are just the start of 3i's ambitious plans to harness the vast amount of information and knowledge that is created, on a daily basis within the company.

The backing of senior management, particularly Richard Summers, the previous head of Group Services, led to the implementation of MIDAS, which is now accessible to all staff. This is an electronic library that has become a mission-critical tool for the investment teams that negotiate 3i's investments.

Plans for a 3i intranet are also underway, to facilitate more communication and knowledge sharing throughout the company.

Results

MIDAS, although only an internal directory in electronic format, allows all 3i staff full access to company contacts. It also enables mail shots according to user classification. MIDAS contains around 20,000 companies and 40,000 individuals, including the current 3,200 companies in the 3i portfolio.

Knowledgebase, in its simplest form, is a large, corporate database which allows the use and dissemination of corporate knowledge. This is the accumulated knowledge and experience of the 3i industry advisers based near Birmingham. The database is categorised by industry sector and subsequently by company, size, turnover, together with market overviews, broker reports, and other information. It is the responsibility of the industry adviser to carry out their visits and then to enter their findings on to the Knowledgebase.

Internally, the development of the Knowledgebase has allowed a greater flexibility of resources than ever before. With the ownership of content falling firmly on the shoulders of the industry advisers, projecting knowledge becomes a responsibility without which the investment teams cannot operate. The Knowledgebase has helped to speed up delivery, as well as bringing the investment teams up to speed in areas in which they may previously have had little or no knowledge. The feedback on this new system has been extremely positive and has greatly reduced the need for paperwork between offices.

Some recent feedback suggests real enthusiasm for 'Watson' rather than mere compliance:

(The ID Knowledgebase is) fantastic, terrific, a very nice piece of kit. Just what we need when we have to meet a customer for the first time and appear more intelligent than we are!

John Holden, 3i Bristol

This is a good example of 'spreading the knowledge' around 3i.

Richard Bishop, 3i Nottingham

. . . a significant step forward in better sharing the knowledge we have within 3i.

David Brister, 3i Cambridge

Such feedback highlights two key issues. Investment teams at 3i are made up of extremely bright and hard-working people. However, with the complexities of business and commerce today, there is only so much that one person can know at any one given time. Knowledgebase allows the transfer of knowledge to such individuals, allowing them to acquire knowledge created in another part of the organisation, quickly and efficiently. Time and access to this knowledge is no longer an issue, as it is available at any time or location.

Key Learnings

Smoother and more flexible working relationships are vital across the organisation to make knowledge mobilisation happen.

Successful knowledge sharing can only come about through an organisation-wide recognition that the capture of knowledge, and its subsequent dissemination, are vital for smoother and more flexible working relationships.

Senior executives at 3i have long understood that networking is crucial to their business. However, the company needed to extend the reach of these personal and individual networks to a greater level of detail, and throughout the organisation.

The recognition and acceptance that a knowledge-intensive business must harness knowledge is a prerequisite for successful knowledge transfer. At 3i, MIDAS and Knowledgebase have initiated a successful move to project knowledge beyond the level of the individual.

Contact Details

Charles Richardson
Director of Corporate Affairs
Tel: +44 (0)171 928 3131

Andersen Consulting

Situation

In the late 1980s, businesses and other organisations began to tap into the potential of the information highway as a way of revolutionising the way poeple work and do business. Andersen Consulting recognised they could meet clients' need faster and more effectively if staff could access information resources on-line, where and when they needed them. Most importantly, clients would benefit from the collective knowledge of the whole organisation worldwide, and from Andersen Consulting's experience in diverse industries and competencies.

The Challenge

This vision led to the creation of the Knowledge Xchange knowledge management system in 1992. The Knowledge Xchange system provides Andersen Consulting's professionals with universal access to organisation-wide knowledge and experience.

A key advantage of the Knowledge Xchange system is in the area of core knowledge: the proven, innovative approaches to business challenges that consultants adapt to client requirements. The organisation created a shared repository of Andersen Consulting's best industry practices (industry visions, best practices and business process models); methods (integrated sets of methodology building blocks, work objects, job aids and other tools); and leading-edge technology information. In addition, clients benefit from the consultants' ability to obtain advice from Andersen Consulting experts anywhere in the world, to join electronic discussions to exchange ideas and solve problems, to search external newsfeeds and industry analyses and to identify colleagues with special skills.

This vast storehouse of knowledge organises the firm's accumulated experience into accessible knowledge bases that are integrated with Andersen Consulting's Solution Planning process. Reinvention is minimised, allowing teams to focus on crafting custom solutions. These refined approaches can then be captured by the system to assist future clients.

The goal is that – because consultants have ready access to the organisation's accumulated knowledge base and wealth of specialists – they are equipped to provide the best solutions to particular client needs quickly. The system is designed to transfer knowledge efficiently so that users can share their expertise with colleagues while remaining focused on their own client responsibilities.

What Happened

A Global Community.

At its most basic level, the Knowledge Xchange system architecture provides a global communications infrastructure for the organisation. The system is based on standardised hardware and software – including desktop and portable PCs, software for e-mail, groupware, word processing, spreadsheets and presentations – with custom-developed applications, architectures and tools.

The Knowledge Xchange system connects consultants on engagement sites with office-based personnel – it links partners, managers and staff. Less tangibly, it fosters a sense of community that can be hard to achieve in a widely dispersed organisation. Its groupware capability allows users to establish on-line relationships with other Andersen Consulting personnel working on similar projects. This creates a virtual 'place' in which users exchange ideas, collaborate on solutions, and share documents such as work plans and presentations.

The Results

Andersen Consulting believes it is the first business to succeed in building a global, internetworked Lotus Notes environment to manage its information resources. Its unique network of Local Area Networks (LANs) enables it to replicate data around the world and provide users in 47 nations with real-time access to servers around the world. When used in concert with its voice network and video-conferencing abilities, Andersen Consulting believes that the Knowledge Xchange system effectively erases the boundaries of time and geography, enabling the global organisation to work together as one.

Key Learnings

Design of the Knowledge Xchange System.
In designing the Knowledge Xchange system, Andersen Consulting sought to leverage its greatest resources: its people and the knowledge they have built. In building an information infrastructure, it made a concerted effort to gather opinions worldwide. Andersen Consulting is a complex, multicultural organisation of operating units matrixed with global communities of practice, each with their own needs and priorities. Taking this into account, the Knowledge Xchange system aims to balance the needs of operating units and communities with the enterprise-wide need for coherence and standards. The result is an on-line "information neighbourhood" in which knowledge capital is captured, stored, enhanced and shared across the organisation.

Like other types of capital, knowledge capital depreciates over time. It loses its usefulness if not kept up to date. For that reason knowledge management is a priority within Andersen Consulting to ensure ongoing quality. Automating the dissemination of information resources has resulted in their increased use by staff and their integration into business processes worldwide.

It was recognised from the beginning that this system represents a new way of working. As helpful as the system is, it requires that personnel adopt new work habits and integrate system use into their daily lives. To help people adjust to their new electronic neighbourhood, they are offered on-line "guided tours" to major applications as well as more traditional training approaches. Internal marketing efforts include newsletters devoted to helping new users get oriented and make the most of the system. Some of the new applications are tested in the Usability Testing Lab, obtaining input from a variety of users. Policies for system use have been established that provide needed structure, such as standards for global knowledge sharing.

These efforts have been rewarded by steady growth in the number of users and the extent to which they use the system. More than 51,000 users (more than 85 percent of the Andersen Consulting staff) currently have access to the system and use it daily for communicating and on an as-needed basis for sharing knowledge. The goal is to get every staff-member to integrate the Knowledge Xchange system into their daily work routines.

Benefits of a Knowledge Management System.
Andersen Consulting recommends that every knowledge-based organisation interested in maintaining a competitive edge in the marketplace should consider investing in a knowledge manage-ment system. They believe it is one of the most important strategic moves an organisation can make toward providing the best service to its customers. Using the Knowledge Xchange system as a model, they also help clients build their own systems so that their businesses can take full advantage of their own knowledge capital.

The Knowledge Xchange system continually and vividly demonstrates its usefulness and value. For example, a consultant can help a client target areas of strength and opportunities for improvement, comparing performance against current data from industry competitors. A consultant can identify where the expertise lies in the organisation for the job within minutes. A consultant wrestling with a programming challenge can get time-saving advice from colleagues who have already solved the same problem – colleagues who are halfway around the world. Users constantly report that the Knowledge Xchange system has enabled them to work more effectively.

For Andersen Consulting, the system is a necessary step toward the 'virtual office' that they see reshaping their business environment in the global arena. The organisation is already moving toward just-in-time offices to optimise use of space and to reduce commuting. With the Knowledge Xchange system in place, teleworking professionals need only a computer, a modem and bandwidth to access all the resources they require to do their jobs.

Further efficiencies are being realised in the area of training. In the past, Andersen Consulting staff have travelled from around the world to the training facilities. With more than 59,000 personnel, new methods of training are necessary. Classroom instruction is supplemented with automated, multimedia courses that can be delivered on demand and are available over the network. The Knowledge Xchange system is also used to distribute updated training information quickly and cost-effectively.

Future Growth

In time, as bandwidth increases, the Knowledge Xchange system will become even more robust. Andersen Consulting will be in a position to deliver multimedia data to end users, which will make the exchange of information more powerful. Users will be able to access larger data items and enjoy substantially faster access to knowledge bases. Overall, they plan to continue and improve the integration of the internal system with external services as new options become available.

Contact Details:

Janice E. Reid
Knowledge Manager
Global Knowledge Management
Operating Group " UK & Ireland RMG
Tel: +44 (0)171 304 8732
E-mail: janice.e.reid@ac.com

APTV

Background

APTV is the video news-gathering arm of the Associated Press. APTV began its first world-wide news bulletins on Sunday, 13 November 1994, starting the latest stage of its development into the most comprehensive news service in the world.

APTV's sole mission is to provide television broadcasters with unrivalled news video footage. Its service covers the world's top stories every day, with a special emphasis on the most important stories for each region. APTV is a strategic part of AP's overall plan to provide a comprehensive array of news-gathering services for its customers. The company uses the judgement and expertise of AP, but has hired experienced television professionals to manage assignments, work the cameras, edit gear and co-ordinate satellite operations.

Context

In the summer of 1996, APTV introduced Lotus Notes as a response to a number of information-related problems within the organisation. The Director of Marketing, Michael Liebreich, says that the organisation had a poor history of point-to-point communication, and Daryl Staehle, Director of Sales and Customer Relations, refers to the organisation's information structure as a 'bucket brigade': each person's bucket added more unstructured information to an already overloaded system.

APTV staff relied on three databases, Contacts, Bureaus and Organisations. Obviously, different users and departments had different information requirements. However, it was felt that the three databases were not fulfilling the needs of the whole organisation effectively. The integrity of the databases was constantly being questioned, in terms of content and structure; duplication across the databases had created an unmanageable plethora of customer contact details. Users were rarely sure that the information they had was correct and up-to-date. Indeed, many staff had taken to running their own databases on electronic personal organisers.

With its simple electronic mail and ability to track customer enquiries, Lotus Notes seemed the simple and ideal solution. It would allow APTV's Regional Executives constant access to the databases when travelling, and would facilitate e-mail contact without having to stay on-line in areas with poor communication links.

The Challenge

The three existing databases had to be integrated into one database on Notes. This would enable people to 'share buckets' in a managed and organised fashion.

APTV has always gone to great lengths to state its commitment to produce the best service possible. This means meeting the needs of the customers it already served, as well as those of the new customers that were to join the organisation.

Customer service, an often stated business objective, was vital to APTV when entering the fiercely competitive and changing sector of television news. It was crucial for the company's expertise to be passed on as the organisation grew.

What Happened?

Notes was sponsored at board level and the project went ahead with a suitable budget set aside for training and hardware upgrades.

The three databases were duly merged and the resulting 'new' database went through a major clean-up to ensure that the earlier errors and duplication were removed. The biggest challenge was to design a user interface that was 'friendly', but similar to the interface on the old Contacts, Bureaus and Organisations databases.

The existing e-mail system was scrapped and Notes users were introduced to the software with great success. All users were trained so that the training was completed just before they received their user IDs.

Results

Notes has allowed a higher level of staff contribution than was previously possible. It has also improved the exchange of news and information between departments. Notes technology has enabled Production to know what is going on in Sales and Marketing, for example, and vice-versa. The Communications and Engineering departments no longer have to rely on word-of-mouth communication to learn about new customers. Notes makes the sharing of this information and knowledge easy.

Since the clean-up was completed, communication has not only improved within and across departments, but also between APTV head office in London and its Regional Executives in the USA, Hong Kong and Latin America. These Regional Executives have remote access to the Notes system, irrespective of where they may be. Their example has encouraged user participation across the organisation.

This new and improved level of communication has allowed APTV staff to achieve their stated aim of improving customer service; initial approaches are followed up with visits and telephone calls that are recorded on the database. Sales and Marketing can now be proactive in targeting potential new clients.

Finally, the success of the original system, primarily supporting the Sales and Marketing function, has led to the creation of additional databases within Notes for Communications, Specials and Customers.

Key Learnings

Customer service is vital to the competitive television news sector.

Changing an existing information system requires support from the very top.

Anja Hannusch, APTV's Notes champion, believes that there are many lessons to be learnt from their experience:

1. Changing an existing information system requires support from the very top. The visible support lent to the entire project by Michael Liebreich helped to ensure that users were enthusiastic about Notes before it was launched.

2. A staggered roll-out enables potential users to become familiar with Notes on their colleagues' computers before they have it installed on their own machines.

3. The staff were given external training before being allowed to access Notes in the office. When the training was completed, they were then given access to the new e-mail system. This enabled users to get a feel for what was essentially a new piece of software. By the time Notes was ready to be rolled-out to users, they were already familiar with it.

4. When an organisation-wide initiative is underway, people look to a 'champion' for support. APTV's Notes

champion, Anja Hannusch, may have fought a lonely battle at times, but her efforts in ensuring the successful take-up of Notes have proved that every project requires a designated head whom people can turn to for help and advice.

Contact Details

Anja Hannusch
Marketing Associate
E-mail:anja-hannusch@ap.org

Michael Liebreich
Director of Marketing & Strategic Planning
E-mail:michael-liebreich@ap.org

Head Office
Tel: +44 (0) 171 427 4000

Blue Curve Ltd

Background

Blue Curve was formed by Mark Robertson, a former employee of SBC Warburg. Swiss Bank Corporation is one of its major clients.

Context

In the spring of 1994, Swiss Bank Corporation identified an area where technology, in this case a combination of Lotus Notes and an intranet, could play a role in releasing information that its people created. Financial research in investment banks is presented as analyst-type reports that are sent out to financial investors. The reputation of the bank can rest on the quality and accuracy of the reports. It is not only clients who rely on this information, but also in-house specialists from a wide range of departments.

The Challenge

All investment banks churn out mountains and mountains of paper, much of which is duplicated in one form or another. Analyst reports, for example, generally start out as MS Word documents which are formatted by editors. The printers then add colour and the finishing touches, so we have a process where three sets of people have worked on one report. With an intranet as a front-end resource, no such formatting is required.

The 'mailing list' syndrome is a big cultural issue here. On the whole, people are very reluctant to put out information into cyberspace. The issue of trust plays a key role; information providers do not know who will use their material and information users do not know the source of their information.

What Happened?

Blue Curve developed a system called 'Swiss View' for SBC which is, in essence, a picture of what is happening in the world's financial markets. It is used throughout SBC and has fundamentally changed the entire research function. It no longer matters who has produced the information that the end user accesses as the information is constantly updated: it is a very mature system.

Lotus Notes is used as a process-modelling system. It is used to handle processes and workflow – essentially a back-end technology. The intranet site is used by traders and sales staff using a Netscape browser. The Notes system is responsible for disseminating information through the whole organisation, as well as providing a 'virtual private network' for fifty or so clients.

Results

Blue Curve is making its Research Net available to investment banks internationally. Using Notes and internet technology, the system is a collection and dissemination system for the vast amount of information that banks produce on a daily basis. It also effectively removes the need to contact someone personally – an analyst in Tokyo may be in bed when a colleague in London requires information that was produced a few hours earlier. Research Net is categorised into four areas (acting as a suitable and efficient knowledge map):

- Company
- Sector

- Country
- Region

All information is tagged with one or more categories. Documents are then published according to their categorisation. This allows for a more structured approach internally and in collating information in the investment banking area.

Key Learnings

The next battle is to eliminate paper!
Notes is a back-end aid to production, allowing information to be tagged, indexed and ordered.

Contact Details

Mark Robertson
Managing Director
Tel: +44 (0) 171 929 8300

Buckman Laboratories International, Inc.

Background

Buckman Laboratories' key to success is its expert knowledge of water treatment and similar processes. It prides itself on collaborating closely with customers, understanding their needs in depth and creating the best solutions. Electronic communication has enhanced this collaboration by bringing Buckman's global expertise to where it matters most – the customer interface.

Buckman Laboratories is one of the few examples of both the Chairman and CEO taking personal responsibility for knowledge. Robert H. Buckman was the Chairman of the Board at Buckman Laboratories International until late 1996 and is now the Chairman of the Board of Bulab Holdings Inc.

Context

The move to create Buckman Laboratories' 'community of one' – expanding the power of associates through increasing their range of communication – started over ten years ago. Buckman recognised early on that the greatest knowledge base in the company would not be found in a computer database but in the heads of the associates. Over 72 per cent of the company's associates possess a university or college degree.

Bob Buckman admitted that the challenge facing the organisation was to get each individual to share what they know, freely and openly, with others. How could Buckman Laboratories get each individual to assume responsibility for their actions? Where should the focus lie?

The Challenge

An analysis of working practices at Buckman Laboratories found that, at any given moment, 86 per cent of the company's associates were out of the office in any one of ninety different countries. As associates spend less than 14 per cent of their available time in the office, it seems logical to conclude that the office is not the place where business takes place.

A further realisation was that the cash flow of the company is not generated in the office; it is generated on the front-line with the customer. It is only by closing the gap with the customer, on the front-line, that the business will benefit. It seemed necessary, therefore, to redefine 'the office' and re-create it where the work of the company is done.

The obstacles to success, as in most organisations, were the typical structure of hierarchical organisations, geographical spread, language, and cultural barriers. Management at Buckman Laboratories focused the entire company on breaking down these existing barriers.

The power of the individual to communicate with others in the organisation was very important to achieving success. Most companies that gather information on the front-line have a system for directing this information upwards; several people will add their own perspective before a 'guru' at the top of the organisation gives the information the benefit of his infinite wisdom. When the originator sees the information again, they often do not recognise it, or it does not communicate what was intended. The confusion could be eliminated by letting the person who needs the knowledge talk directly to those with the latest and best knowledge.

Bob Buckman knew he needed to increase the range of communication of the associates, helping them to change the organisation and increase its power in the marketplace. By allowing them to talk to each other directly, the company could move towards providing an instant response to the customer.

What Happened?

Bob Buckman cites culture change as the most difficult aspect of knowledge transfer to achieve: 'The climate that we create as leaders has a major impact on our ability to share knowledge across time and space.'

People traditionally hoard knowledge. They have been taught that hoarding knowledge can achieve power. For most of us, our school years taught us how to acquire and use knowledge; we did not learn to share it. Today's business environment requires us to reverse that tendency. 'The most powerful individuals will be those that become a source of knowledge by proactively sharing what they have or what they can get their hands on.' It is a stated company objective that: A climate of continuity and trust is vital to accomplish proactive knowledge sharing within the company, this being the same climate of continuity and trust that Buckman Laboratories wishes to create with its customers.'

This relationship with customers is built by people – in this case, the associates on the front-line. Applications experts and industry specialists can be involved at the customer interface level provided they are *effectively engaged on the front-line*. The number of people in the organisation working on this relationship with the customer, relative to the total organisation, will determine the momentum of the organisation.

Senior management at Buckman Laboratories has laid down an organisation-wide objective to have 80 per cent of the company effectively engaged on the front-line by the year 2000.

What does this mean?

The company states: 'Effective engagement happens when an associate takes responsibility for, and is actively involved with, satisfying the needs and expectations of our customers, so that Buckman Laboratories becomes the preferred choice.'

Mike Anstey, an associate from the Canadian office, described in an on-line Forum discussion the difficulty of putting this objective into practice: 'How do we get as many people as possible creating and transferring as much knowledge as possible in order to have a positive impact on the customer?'

This requires involvement, creativity, commitment, passion and the freedom to explore every opportunity; it must use all available knowledge to make sure that the company has done its utmost to satisfy the customer. It is essential to connect the collection of minds that exist within the company across structural, geographic, cultural and language barriers. There is a need to transfer knowledge effectively across time and space to meet the needs of customers.

Results

Buckman Laboratories introduced a new communication strategy, known as K'NetixSM, or the Buckman Knowledge Network, as the first step in accelerating knowledge transfer and knowledge sharing within the company. As a beginning, they developed a network infrastructure that provided access from around the world, using the on-line CompuServe network. This enabled the network to be created in less than one month. Much of the initial CompuServe activity has been placed on to the company intranet (K'NetixSM). The network allows for the development of on-line forums; it houses a knowledge information centre plus libraries of frequently requested information. Future activities include developing an on-line 'university', redefining the organisation around the flow of information and accelerating the development of key people.

From 1988 to 1992, the average sale of products less than five years old was 22.2 per cent of total sales. In the next four years, it was 32.9 per cent. Buckman Laboratories attributes this difference to the improved ability to communicate and share knowledge across the organisation. With K'NetixSM, Buckman Laboratories is able to close the gap with the customer 50 per cent faster than before, creating enormous competitive value for the company. Response times have fallen from days and weeks to a couple of hours – at the most a day or two. This is particularly important at the furthest reaches of the company. It makes no difference how close you are to the home office; the response time is the same anywhere in the world.

People who are capable of influencing others in the company have a larger audience today as their range of influence is much greater. These are the people who are ultimately picked for advancement and promotion. Talent has therefore flourished with a resultant increase in morale.

Closer customer contact and feedback has led to increased innovation on the front-line, making a further difference to the company's competitive edge. Buckman Laboratories monitors the percentage of sales from products that are less than five years old; the organisation knows that it is closing the gap with the customer if this percentage is high.

Each department has a very clear role: the front-line defines the need, R&D has to create or find the products, Manufacturing has to produce them or arrange for their production and Sales has to complete the circle with the customer on the front-line. This cycle takes the relationships of continuity and trust throughout the company as well as with the customer. The entire company must be involved if the percentage is to remain high. The higher the percentage, the faster the company can move to satisfy the needs of its customers.

Key Learnings

The most powerful individuals will be those who become a source of knowledge.

The knowledge base is the cumulative knowledge and brainpower of the organisation.

Each organisation is inherently different. It serves different purposes, has different needs and employs many different types of people. However, every organisation has a knowledge base that is the cumulative knowledge and brain power of the whole organisation. Recognising this, and transferring this knowledge into an accessible resource, requires a careful analysis of the work patterns of these knowledge bearers, the culture within the organisation and the other barriers that are likely to impede such a movement.

The sheer drive and inspiration of the associates has made knowledge accessible at any time, anywhere within Buckman Laboratories. The resultant improvement in customer service and commitment to customers serves to highlight the importance of knowledge leadership: setting the direction, communicating the benefits, and above all, leading by example. Bob Buckman has demonstrated all these qualities through his work on K'NetixSM.

The Buckman Laboratories Code of Ethics has played an important part in gelling together the constituent parts of the company. It provides the basis for the respect and trust that are necessary in a knowledge-sharing environment. These fundamental beliefs are essential to communicating across the many barriers that exist in any organisation.

Finally, the leadership of Bob Buckman and the Code of Ethics act as a reminder to the staff that knowledge sharing comes about only through radical, yet slow, change. Such changes become the norm for any organisation that wishes to achieve a successful knowledge sharing environment.

Contact Details

Bob Buckman
Chairman of the Board
Bulab Holdings Inc
  Tel: 001 901 272 8240
  E-mail: rhbuckman@buckman.com
NOTE: K'NetixSM is a service mark of Buckman Laboratories International Inc.

Burson-Marsteller

Background

Burson-Marsteller describes itself as a Global Perception Management Firm. It describes itself as a 'Knowledge-Based People Business', focusing on delivering measurable business results to its clients through a full range of consulting and communications disciplines.

The company was founded over forty years ago by Harold Burson and Bill Marsteller in a single office in the United States. Burson-Marsteller now has its headquarters in New York and has 2,200 professionals working from 76 offices in 35 countries on five continents. It enjoys a strong presence in every major business centre in the world. In 1996, the company earned more than $265 million in net fees. Burson-Marsteller forms part of the Young & Rubicam Inc. family of companies.

Burson-Marsteller serves a diverse body of clients ranging from multi-national corporations, through business organisations and professional associations to governmental bodies and not-for-profit institutions. Its functional and industry practice areas include healthcare, marketing, advertising and creative services, media, public affairs and technology.

Context

The company strategy focuses on its key global clients; the company is committed to serving the clients' needs whenever and wherever they arise. The mission statement reveals that a relentless pursuit of exceptional value for clients is the goal of all activities. Every structure within the organisation – its practice emphasis on professional development, the presence in major global markets for local implementation and its expert creative and strategic resource groups – is dedicated to support the clients and the client leaders around the world. At the heart of this strategy, knowledge is playing a critical role as the deliverer of global value and the symbol of the global professional power which the firm promises its clients.

Achieving 15 per cent annual growth calls for an investment in knowledge management capabilities which can overcome the firm's size and organisational complexity, freeing the various pockets of expertise that are developing within the organisation. The added benefit of Burson-Marsteller's knowledge strategy is the provision of consistent, quality service to clients across geographical boundaries.

The Challenge

Creating a knowledge culture and a knowledge-sharing company required effort and commitment from both staff and management. Knowledge was to be the driver which differentiated Burson-Marsteller from its competitors; management recognised the role that technology would play in bringing different parts of the organisation together.

Linking the knowledge and insight of Burson-Marsteller's employees, both philosophically and electronically, required complete participation from the end user. They were needed to help channel company resources into areas where the technological solution would become a daily part of the business user's life. The company had to find a way of integrating this insight and knowledge into a company-wide, organisation-specific technical solution. Sharing information would be a critical part of this new system.

The solution was to allow end users to access and share information across and within practices or countries, using a common 'language'. The ultimate aim was to make knowledge gathering and sharing easier.

What Happened?

In 1995, Burson-Marsteller started creating a knowledge sharing culture (with knowledge primarily defined as the methods and tools which have evolved through client work). The company had two clear objectives: the first was to identify, organise and share knowledge widely; the second was to create and maintain a consistent quality of knowledge-based products and services. Over time, a third objective evolved which had been implied before but was now made explicit: the increased profession-alisation of the client team by providing added-value information services as a direct input to the client work.

As a beginning, one person in each market was made respons-ible for redistributing client information and making it usable. The knowledge specialist was also entrusted with becoming the person responsible for desk research, the learning and utilisation of on-line information services and the input into the growing Lotus Notes-based databases. At the time, this was the largest application of Lotus Notes within the Young & Rubicam organisation. The knowledge network allowed users access to databases containing information on markets, clients, audiences and topical issues. By 1996, this had evolved into a new system which ensured that people at Burson-Marsteller were not duplicating previous research and assignments. The new system had common standards, networks and practices.

Results

The result was 'InfoDesk', Burson-Marsteller's own Information and Knowledge Management System. It consists of more than forty Lotus Notes databases that users can access from their desktops. InfoDesk allows the capture and organisation of information and allows the global organisation to share its knowledge easily. It was rolled out in the world in 1996 and 1997.

InfoDesk enables the user to research expertise throughout the company at very short notice. It also provides a vehicle for finding Burson-Marsteller experts and expertise through employee profiles on the HR databases. The groupware functionality of Lotus Notes allows individuals to keep track of and manage a new business opportunity. Additions and amendments to a project can easily be recorded from start to finish.

Standard templates for client presentations mean that the consultant is able to tailor the entire presentation to the client's requirements within minimum fuss and effort. Moreover, it enables the organisation to use the power of world-wide insights without always having to move people around. The groupware capability reinforces the firm's cultural bias towards collaborative work, by enabling dislocated client team members to operate as one team through InfoDesk.

Training the business users was crucial to the successful uptake of InfoDesk, so each and every business user was provided with a thorough introduction to InfoDesk before they were allowed access to the system.

InfoDesk has allowed Burson-Marsteller to deliver better value to clients through more efficient practice management. It has also allowed, and on occasions forced, better communication between staff across borders, be they departmental or geographical. Furthermore, it has resulted in a better use of the Burson-Marsteller network and its resources. Most importantly, it has allowed bright and innovative professional people to win new business by using existing knowledge.

Recent developments on InfoDesk include access to the Internet, real-time monitoring of external news from world-wide publications or newswires, and creation of a 'centre of excellence' where the best ideas, work and offering are publicised in order to generate innovation. In addition to the Lotus version, users can now access InfoDesk from the net and from within the Y&R intranet. Management is also considering connecting the internal system to their client's own intranets through an extranet.

Key Learnings

Achieving a knowledge culture requires effort and commitment from both staff and management.

User involvement and participation are vital to make it work.

To create a more open, sharing culture – to make InfoDesk work – user involvement and participation are vital. The endorsement of senior managers is crucial to encourage executives to use the intranet and to contribute to it. Identifying 'champions' who can provide local help, support, explanation and communication was a key to the success of InfoDesk in remote markets such as Eastern Europe or the Far East. The addition of newcomers to the company contributed greatly to the success of InfoDesk: older members of the company took little interest in InfoDesk because they thought they already knew everything, but new employees were thrilled to have such an immediate and powerful tool at hand.

Beyond InfoDesk, one has to consider Burson-Marsteller's global knowledge management strategy. InfoDesk is one of many tools and processes that the company has developed to enhance knowledge creation and sharing. A more in-depth programme, addressing the need to tackle tacit knowledge, has since been undertaken under the leadership of the Chief Knowledge Officer.

Contact Details

Richard C. Powell Jr
VP/Director, Global Information Management
Tel: +1 212 614 4592
E-mail: *richard-powell@bm.com*

Stephanie Bonnet
Knowledge Network Manager/Europe

Tel: +44 (0) 171 931 6262
E-mail:*stephanie-bonnet@bm.com*

Hertha Meyer
Knowledge Network Manager/Asia-Pacific
Tel: +65 331 5274
E-mail: *hertha-meyer@bm.com*

Ernst & Young

Background

In the worlds of accountancy and management consultancy, Ernst & Young needs little introduction. It is one of the 'Big Five' accountancy companies with a world-wide staff of approximately 79,000 people, it has 676 offices in 130 countries. It is one of the world's largest audit, tax and consultancy firms. In the UK, Ernst & Young has 6,600 professional staff in 24 offices; they offer a whole range of services: audit, accounting, insolvency, consultancy, corporate finance and many others. In 1997, Ernst & Young had an annual revenue of $9.1 billion.

Context

Ernst & Young is a huge world-wide organisation. Even within the UK, the effective management of information, for a professional staff of over 6,000, has become an onerous task.

Ernst & Young's knowledge management initiatives started four years ago. They were driven by a business need and, as a result, the organisation as a whole has made headway into knowledge sharing which goes beyond the conceptual.

In the UK, increased competition and stricter regulation has meant that accountancy practices have been forced to 'add value' to clients more than ever before. In order to remain competitive, teamwork and knowledge sharing have become the vehicles for additional 'value-added' business.

The Challenge

According to Knowledge Management Manager, Liz de Freitas, the challenge has been enormous. For an organisation the size of Ernst & Young, even just in the UK, moving to a knowledge sharing culture implies a huge change for all involved. Breaking down existing barriers is a prerequisite to creating an environment where professionals readily exchange the information and knowledge that was once the key to their status and their ticket to upward mobility through the organisation.

The appointment of Tim Curry as the UK Chief Knowledge Officer heralded the organisation's commitment to build on the initiatives already underway in the US. The aim was to create a culture of knowledge sharing that would ultimately benefit the end customer, the Ernst & Young client.

In the US, the consultancy arm of the organisation had driven the move to share knowledge. In the UK, however, the equivalent programme started with the audit function, because of an awareness that leveraging the knowledge of all employees worldwide was a prerequisite for audit innovation. The challenge of meeting the ever-increasing needs of clients led senior management at Ernst & Young to recognise that managing the company's knowledge effectively was critical in gaining a competitive advantage over its competitors.

The challenges facing Ernst & Young, therefore, were both organisational – due to the size and complexity of the UK practice – and also individual: attempting to overcome the 'Why should I bother?' syndrome.

Ernst & Young has recognised that mobilising its audit knowledge requires tapping the knowledge of all its audit practitioners world-wide. With this in mind, technology would play an important link in this process of connecting the client handlers to 'high' value knowledge. However, Tim Curry and his team understood that, before the right technology was in place, the organisation needed to overcome the issue of cultural change. Only when these barriers were overcome would technology be a useful enabler for effective knowledge sharing.

What Happened?

Tim Curry heads up a team of Knowledge Officers. His team are the sponsors or champions of the process in each department. There may be more than one Knowledge Officer assigned to a given department if it is particularly large.

A Global Steering committee was formed, made up of Ernst & Young businesses from ten countries. Tim Curry sits on this committee to ensure that the world-wide organisation is working together to co-ordinate its knowledge management initiatives.

In the UK, the team of Knowledge Officers works closely with the research teams in each department to provide knowledge services to the entire practice. It is the duty of the Knowledge Officers to identify the knowledge needs of the business, then set and support relevant objectives.

Results

The UK knowledge management team focused first on selected business units, including Financial and Energy Services. The team collected and generated knowledge about Ernst & Young's work in these areas and built a contact database about its customers. The success of these projects sent an important signal to the rest of the organisation: managing the collective knowledge of the organisation provided a valuable and tangible benefit to the client. It also enabled Ernst & Young to cut costs, especially in terms of duplicating research in these areas.

Ernst & Young now has a Lotus Notes infrastructure as part of its corporate intranet; this is known as the 'Knowledge Web'. It contains best practice databases, external databases, document repositories and informal discussion databases. All of these databases are owned and actively managed to ensure quality of content. Access to the Knowledge Web is gained through a catalogue that uses a global navigation taxonomy, creating consistency and facilitating global sharing.

Ernst & Young split up its knowledge management approach into three key areas – Culture, Content and Technology. 'Culture' encompasses the Ernst & Young vision of knowledge management; it includes achieving competitive advantage through knowledge sharing, raising the firm's profile and making knowledge sharing a highly visible pervasive practice. New recruits undergo knowledge training as part of their induction, embedding the process as more than just a concept. Communication and awareness is emphasised: the two encourage behavioural change and, ultimately, lead to an improved offering to clients.

The 'Content' determines what is made available to Ernst & Young staff to help them fulfil their business objectives. 'PowerPacks' are Notes databases that house internal information, best practices, exemplary deliverables and thought leadership.

'Technology' falls under the management of the IT and IS functions of the organisation. They ensure that the networks and Notes infrastructure are running efficiently and smoothly, with little disruption to the end user in the business.

The three areas are inextricably linked and constitute the basis for knowledge management at Ernst & Young. The activities of the teams that mange each area are 'rooted in creating valuable content, creating processes to collect, update, store, add value and deploy knowledge, and in training our people in the technologies, processes and content.' The response from the business units has been favourable and close ties have been established between knowledge teams in the US and in the UK.

Key Learnings

Teamwork and knowledge have become the vehicles for 'value-added' business.

Integrate knowledge sharing into training and development processes.

John Peetz is now Ernst & Young's world-wide CKO. This is how he sums up his objective:

> To create an effective knowledge sharing culture, organisations must champion the cause of the knowledge process, integrate knowledge sharing into training and staff development processes, constantly communicate and promote internally, celebrate successes and establish a clearly defined infrastructure which everyone in the organisation understands. Our infrastructure includes process owners, executive steering committees and knowledge creators and integrators.

The UK practice has recognised the importance of creating a knowledge sharing culture, but it has also recognised that knowledge sharing will continue to take place in organisations informally. What Tim Curry and his team have done is to harness technology to formalise and widen the old networks beyond small departmental teams or practice areas. At the same time, it is still important to encourage client handlers to talk to each other. A larger, more coherent network fulfils Ernst & Young's objective of serving its clients better, while 'adding value' to their business.

Contact Details

Liz de Freitas
Knowledge Management Manager
Tel: +44 (0)171 928 2000

Henley Management College

Background

Henley Management College in Oxfordshire is an independent, international business school. It was founded in 1945 as an Administrative Staff College and has a long-standing record of innovation in management education and development. At present, Henley is one of the UK's largest providers of distance learning; it has more than 6,000 MBA students in Europe, Africa, Hong Kong, Singapore, New Zealand and other distant locations. All distant learning programmes are supported electronically using Lotus Notes.

Context

Henley began its MBA programme over twenty years ago, and in 1984, the College introduced an MBA through 'distance learning'. Its students study either directly with Henley or through one of its international associates. The programme uses a mixture of video and audio materials, workbooks, disk-based materials and regular workshops, and it takes approximately three years to complete the Henley MBA.

Information and communication technology have revolutionised management education. Some students attend one-week residential courses at Henley, but for most, electronic communication is their only means of connection to a global network of fellow MBA students.

The Challenge

Encouraging collaboration in any environment is difficult. At Henley, this difficulty was intensified by the geographical diversity of its student body. Through its residential programmes, Henley encourages an informal dialogue between students from different industries and countries. With over 6,000 students globally, and associate organisations in twenty countries world-wide, the school has to provide an environment that allows for the same level of interaction among its non-residential students.

During the late 1980s, Henley recognised that information technology could be a major driver of change in the management education market. However, any technological solution had to be able to cross the boundaries of time and space, allowing students to work together on group projects. It also had to allow students to work at their own pace. Most importantly, bearing in mind the educational context of this situation, it had to enhance the learning experience of all students, allowing them to gain insights and knowledge useful in their business careers.

What Happened?

In the summer of 1993, a Lotus Notes project was piloted internally. In the autumn, this was extended to a group of thirty students and, in 1994, the success of the pilots led to Henley's senior management adopting Lotus Notes as part of its distance learning programmes.

The College realised that management education is as much about learning from peers and fellow-students – all of whom have experienced real-life business problems in the workplace – as it is about learning from professors and using academic material. Henley challenged the traditional methods of knowledge sharing within the academic environment, providing its students with an opportunity to discuss current management thinking with a wide range of people. With so many managers taking part in Henley's various programmes, Notes has allowed a structured method for students to benefit from other students.

This global network of MBA students is valuable for several reasons: Professor Colin Carnall, Director of Programmes at Henley, knows that: 'Isolation can be a problem for distance learning students. Local support from partner institutions and a hotline to Henley can help to reduce the loneliness of the long-distance learner. Using Notes, the Henley student can access a world-wide classroom and a high-tech pen-pal register. Students can discuss the finer points of a case study, as well as making contact with people who share common interests or pastimes. And all this can be done without leaving the home or workplace.'

Results

By March 1998, there were over 4,000 students registered and using Lotus Notes. An additional sixty users are going on-line every month. One third of registered users are from outside the UK, spread around countries from India to the Falkland Islands. The 'electronic classroom' enables students such as Gary Bailey, the former England and Manchester United goalkeeper, who did his MBA in South Africa, to become part of a world-wide network.

As long as the student has a suitable computer with a modem, the College provides him or her with a client copy of the Lotus Notes software, as part of the course fee, along with a manual and Notes identity file (ID). Notes allows any student anywhere to dial in to Henley's server, and gain quick, easy access to information, expertise and advice. In addition, Notes allows students to work off-line through asynchronous communication – an important capability since long-distance phone charges make working on-line expensive.

Students have welcomed this electronic form of networking.

One student recently commented that: 'Notes has provided access to colleagues undergoing similar courses of study with similar issues, needs and problems and we can share solutions. It also provides tutorial support quickly and effectively.' Distance is no longer an issue because the help and support provided by Notes is the same. The virtual 'Coffee Room' serves as an informal point to exchange ideas, thoughts and grievances.

Tutors too have welcomed Notes, enabling a 'teleworking faculty', and they have gained additional skills, such as on-line facilitation techniques. As many of the Henley tutors work away from the College, Notes allows easier communication with the College, as well as with the students they are helping. Student queries are responded to in full, providing a one-to-one mini-tutorial, but with the option of other students joining in if they so wish.

Key Learnings

'Virtual' students need the same facilities as 'real' students.

Notes has taken a group of disparate, geographically remote people and shaped them into a community.

Notes has undoubtedly served its purpose of supporting a large, remote student community. It has also served another purpose. New technology is fast becoming an essential part of business life: Notes provides an efficient vehicle for the programme and it is also an effective way of helping people get to grips with modems, groupware and electronic communication.

The College recognises that its success in implementing Notes came about as a result of intensive awareness and training to gain the support of both staff and users. Until the all-important critical mass of users was achieved, persistence and encouragement from Henley staff were vital to keep the databases running. Support from the top of the organisation has been critical to the success of Notes as a knowledge sharing tool.

Notes has provided many wide-ranging benefits; a better solution for communication, support for group work, quick access to key information, a place to turn to for support and mentoring, an aid for programme administration, adoption of a widely-used business technology and, importantly for the investment, a platform for the future.

Contact Details

Fenella Calpin
E-mail: fennellag@henleymc.ac.uk

Professor David Birchall
E-mail: davidbi@henleymc.ac.uk

ICL

Background

ICL is an international company that focuses on helping its clients to seize the opportunities of the information age. Originally, it designed and manufactured computers, but it has been gradually transforming itself into a service-led organisation, making its knowledge of technology a real asset.

Context

This change in direction has made it a strategic imperative for ICL to mobilise its intellectual capital world-wide. Services and methodologies were often duplicated, and there was difficulty in quickly identifying experts to support projects. In some instances, several ICL businesses were bidding separately for the same customer projects without realising it.

The Challenge

ICL needed to improve its information management as well as its ability to understand what tacit knowledge and experience were carried in employees' heads and how to use this know-how more effectively.

ICL has always invested significantly in training and development, focusing on improving the capability of individuals and teams. An equally important focus became the transferring of an employee's or team's skills, knowledge and learning from one part of the organisation to another. In other words, how could ICL add true *organisational* learning to the existing emphasis on training and developing people?

What Happened?

An informal Knowledge Management Network of ICL people who were interested in this challenge came together in late 1994. It was soon realised that knowledge management was already happening informally within the organisation. For example, ICL identified twenty-three internal information services for employees, but, because they were entirely unco-ordinated, there was much duplication across these services. Also, many important activities were being undertaken by isolated individuals, but, unfortunately, by and large, they had insufficient time, money or management support to make a significant difference to the business.

Following a series of workshops in 1995, the Network identified a significant opportunity to accelerate ICL's business transformation, so, in January 1996, the Network recommended that Keith Todd, ICL's new Chief Executive, appoint a full-time Programme Director for a cross-company initiative. Todd accepted the business argument for this, in his first week in the job, and 'Project VIK' (Valuing ICL Knowledge) was born.

During the early weeks of the project, it became clear that the areas in need of most help were people and culture, business processes and technology. It was felt that a small, 'catalyst' team with cross-functional skills would best achieve a clearer understanding of these areas. The team members would need to be change agents, good communicators, effective consultants and influencers. These positions, advertised on ICL's e-mail system, generated 120 responses from fourteen countries. Clearly, the interest and challenge of the project had struck a chord. By mid-1996, a breadth of experience was represented in the new five-person team.

Project VIK was set up deliberately as a project, rather than the separate knowledge management function found in some companies. ICL believed that, as with the quality movement, this important business perspective should be woven into line management responsibilities. The team was, in effect, aiming to make itself redundant rather than to create work for itself.

In the early stages of the project, it was decided to seek easy successes that would be visible across the company, although it was accepted that most of the team's work would be within different management teams and communities. At that local level, it would be possible to evaluate exactly how people, processes and technology needed to change in order to create an effective knowledge sharing environment.

ICL quickly appreciated the opportunities to make knowledge accessible globally provided by new technologies, such as intranets and groupware. Creating a global information service using ICL's intranet was Project VIK's first major target. It was expected to have an immediate impact on productivity by reducing time wasted in locating company information. It was named Café VIK, to reinforce the idea of connecting people.

Results

Client managers estimated that, in the past, they had been spending up to one day every week tracking down information and expertise. If that time could be reduced by half, it would enhance productivity significantly.

With this target in mind, a number of focus groups were run for front-line employees – consultants, project managers and salespeople. ICL asked them what information they needed to do their job more effectively. Although they represented different ICL businesses, some common concerns became clear. They needed information about:

- ICL itself, so that they could be effective ambassadors for the company

- customers and major partners, and ICL's relationships with them
- ICL's services and products
- the processes and policies across the different parts of the company
- the company-wide expertise available to them.

Café VIK became a website on ICL's intranet. It has an attractive design with a cartoon-like character representing the personality of the service. Naturally, he is known as Vik.

By November 1997, its first anniversary, Café VIK was being used by approximately 10,000 of ICL's 19,000 employees. This number continues to grow as awareness of the service spreads.

The benefits of this first step towards being better at 'knowing what we know' have been relayed back in largely anecdotal form. People have been able to identify and contact client managers to alert them to problems or opportunities quickly. Line managers can obtain reliable and up-to-date company policy information. Technical specialists have rapid access to technology briefings, and consultants can use descriptions of capabilities available in other parts of the company in their proposals.

Key Learnings

Take advantage of informal knowledge sharing networks.

The intellectual capital of an organisation is an invisible, but crucial, asset.

The system has one overarching benefit: saving time. This has its own value but, perhaps more importantly, it frees up more time for creating new knowledge.

Now that ICL has learnt more about knowledge sharing, it has become clear that the process needs dedicated support to be effective. The company believes that five main job roles will become increasingly common in organisations that recognise knowledge as a key aspect of competitive advantage. These are:

Chief Knowledge Officer: a member of the senior management team accountable for identifying and mobilising critical knowledge assets. The title is used more widely in the US than in Europe, but the role remains the same.

Information service providers: electronic librarians who organise, catalogue and maintain the knowledge databases. In some organisations, they offer a help desk to search the electronic library for employees. Café VIK is managed by an information services team, without whom data would soon become obsolete, and the value of the service would be diminished in the eyes of users.

Web masters: people responsible for maintaining the technical infrastructure on which information and knowledge is shared. They generally also have responsibility for maintaining an intranet; this role may be combined with that of information service provider.

Knowledge sponsors: people responsible for deciding what knowledge should be shared and presented. For example, a Sales Director might be the knowledge sponsor for the information shared about the clients. S/he would decide if all visits to customers should be followed up by a quick note on the intranet, or whether to increase the number of face-to-face meetings between salespeople in a particular industry. Although not a full-time job, it is a critical role in knowledge-based organisations.

Knowledge owners: a clearly identifiable owner who updates and ensures the accuracy of the system's content. Now that technology makes information so easy to share, most people are knowledge owners and it is critical that this responsibility is taken seriously.

Knowledge owners need to be acquainted with legislation on issues such as data protection and defamation. From ICL's experience, managers should reinforce the importance of this by weaving it into role descriptions and reward and recognition processes.

ICL has built the knowledge perspective into its recruitment, induction, performance management and reward systems. The graduate induction process has a session on the importance of sharing knowledge; the HR function is looking at how to promote knowledge sharing as part of the new psychological contract between the company and its employees. Put simply, ICL wants knowledge sharing to be 'the way we do things around here'.

Keith Todd has expressed a personal vision that everyone in ICL will have the same access to knowledge across the company as he does. By dedicating enthusiastic change agents to this task, ICL is making significant progress. Equally, it has realised that a sustainable knowledge sharing environment needs recognition from every leader in the business, not just the chief executive, and that knowledge is an asset which must be nurtured and protected.

ICL has realised that technology is an enabler of knowledge sharing, but the 'cultural' aspects are the challenge for any organisation in the future. Leadership from the top of the organisation has to be shown visibly and frequently so that people know that giving and receiving knowledge matters to those who matter in the organisation.

Contact Details

Elizabeth Lank
Programme Director, Mobilising Knowledge
Tel: +44 (0) 1753 516000
E-mail: elank@compuserve.com
Note: Thanks are due to People Management magazine for sharing an article from January 1998 about ICL in developing this case study.

Mortgage Express

Background

Mortgage Express was formed in 1986 as a subsidiary of TSB Bank; in May 1997 the company was purchased by Bradford & Bingley Building Society for £64m. The company differs from traditional mortgage providers in that it has no branch network and raises finance directly from the money markets.

The boom in the UK property market saw the company grow rapidly between 1986 and 1990. It attracted 50,000 customers and accumulated mortgage assets of more than £3 billion. However, by the end of 1990, the property market was collapsing and bad debts were accumulating. In 1991 TSB decided to wind up the company within three years.

Despite the continuing recession, however, the company returned to profit in 1993 and, in 1996, it re-entered the mortgage market with a range of popular and innovative products. Mortgage Express currently employs around 350 people at its site in New Barnet, North London. In 1995 it was shortlisted for a UK Quality Award and, the following year, it was a joint winner. The company achieved 'Investor in People' status in 1993 and was the first North London company to be successfully re-accredited in 1996.

Context

The crisis at Mortgage Express began early in 1991 when bad debts and the spectacular decline in the UK housing market caused record losses of more than £70 million. By this time, the company had already stopped taking new mortgages and was expecting to withdraw from the market over the next two to three years.

A new management team, led by Keith Greenough, had taken

over in 1991 to manage the wind-up process. This new team faced a dismal situation. The economy and housing market were in a nose-dive and customers were facing massive losses through negative equity. The old management had been replaced, the business was threatened with closure, and morale amongst Mortgage Express employees was at an all-time low. Staff were not being led effectively and communication between them and management was poor, to say the least. An independent assessment by MORI highlighted this lack of communication at Mortgage Express; in 1991, one member of the staff was quoted as saying: 'I'd like to know what senior management look like!'

The Challenge

The new management team took the view that there was still important work to be done in the interests of the company's stakeholders, although prospects for the company were poor. Communication would be key to achieving this.

The first task was to convince the staff that it was worth putting effort into what looked like a lost cause. The new team made it clear that they could not offer their employees a career, but they would strive to provide an opportunity for people to develop themselves while making Mortgage Express a better company.

At this point, Keith Greenough was quoted as saying to the staff, 'We measure how good the company is by what our stakeholders say – in terms of customer value, in terms of employee perceptions and in terms of returns to the stakeholder. If we succeed, not only will you learn a lot, not only will you gain a lot of positive experience, but – wherever you end up – you will be associated with success.'

Mortgage Express planned to achieve this turnaround using the 'business excellence' model. However, the key challenge was going to be involving its employees and communicating to them that management genuinely wanted to hear their views. Peter

Taylor, Director of HR and Quality, was convinced that employee feedback, and management action from this feedback, would be critical if the company was to turn itself around.

What Happened?

Mortgage Express started the long journey back to profitability by assessing itself against the business excellence model. Management recognised that staff motivation and involvement, backed up by strong internal communications, would form the basis of recovery.

The company started formal communication exercises, including monthly team briefings and departmental communication meetings hosted by managers and attended by directors. In 1996, senior management spent more than 450 working hours in face-to-face meetings; these are encouraged as a means of building trust. Between 1991 and 1995, there were 300 director-led briefings within the company. From the start of the total quality drive, employees at all levels and from all functions trained together. Mortgage Express has worked to build a culture that promotes openness and learning, and encourages knowledge sharing, both formally and informally.

Results

This approach has sent out very strong signals that both management and staff are 'in it together' and that everyone should try to see it through. Barriers have come down and managers have encouraged people to have their say. One way this has been done is through the annual staff opinion survey. Each year, teams review their previous year's progress. The 1996 survey saw record response and satisfaction levels. To quote Peter Taylor, 'People challenge all the time and we encourage that, so that people can be creative about what they do and contribute to improving the company.'

The rationale behind the survey comes from the need to build on feedback from staff. Management are then able to dig down from this data to make comparisons and find trends that provide further feedback; this ensures commitment and ownership from those taking part. These comparisons are not only made between departments but also between external organisations. This 'benchmarking' gives the survey more credibility, allowing Mortgage Express to act in areas where it would not ordinarily have done so.

Meetings over breakfast and afternoon tea send out a clear signal that staff involvement is central to how this business is run, and that an environment of openness and sharing is the norm rather than the exception.

'Project boards' are another visible means of communication to employees. People can find out what is happening in the company, irrespective of department. Project boards increase awareness and provide a visual and open method of promoting the functions and creativity of different departments. 'Our people have a right to understand what the company is doing, where it is going and how it affects them,' states Keith Greenough.

Recognition for the company's efforts in developing its people came with the award of 'Investor in People' status in December 1993 – a significant achievement for an organisation that was then in the process of winding down its business. The recognition of progress in the company reached a pinnacle in 1996 when Mortgage Express were joint winners of the UK Quality Award, awarded by the British Quality Foundation.

Key Learnings

Measure how good your company is by what the stakeholders say.

Build a culture that promotes openness and learning.

Management at Mortgage Express promote the 'employability concept'; each member of staff is given a minimum of five days a year for training and development. They do not receive training for training's sake, but because the company is realistic enough to admit that it cannot guarantee a long-term career to its people. (Mortgage Express has an annual wastage rate of around 12 per cent.) By promoting the 'employability concept', the company takes on the responsibility 'to encourage, enable, facilitate, resource, and recognise continuous development'.

For their part, employees are asked to be flexible, to contribute to their own development, learn continuously as well as to have fun. This has resulted in an organisation where: 'people are able to put their ideas forward and have them listened to,' says Keith Greenough.

The commitment of management at Mortgage Express cannot be overstated. They are ultimately responsible for the open and sharing environment that now exists within the business. They are responsible for focusing the culture on 'communication, communication, communication'. Peter Taylor has no hesitation in saying that: 'It is better to over-communicate than to under-communicate.' If this level of communication can inspire the workforce to work for the good of the company, to achieve, and then improve on this achievement, then management can look back on a job well done. Enabling others to act, and empowering them to do so freely, helps people to achieve their potential. The ultimate beneficiaries are the company stakeholders – the shareholders, the customers and the employees.

Contact Details

Peter Taylor
Director of Human Resources and Quality
Tel: +44 (0)181 449 8888

NCR

Background

NCR is a Fortune 500 company which provides 'Banking Solutions in the Age of the Consumer'. It provides many of the world's main banks with ATMs and the self-service equipment that makes up the consumer interface of the banking business. NCR's main competitors are IBM and, in Europe, Siemens.

NCR's stated mission is to help banks build stronger relationships with their consumers by using its products, knowledge base, expertise and partners to make the consumer interface of the banking business stronger, closer, more flexible and differentiated. Using the latest technology, NCR integrates consumer solutions with the core system of any bank.

NCR Financial Solutions Group (FSG) has its headquarters in London and targets four business functions: self-service solutions, payment solutions, channel-delivery solutions and customer-management solutions, incorporating data warehousing.

Context

NCR's main challenge was to maintain an unrivalled competitive edge. The company decided to meet this challenge head-on; it took a brave decision to share knowledge with chosen companies from its customer base.

Kicki Wallje-Lund, Vice President of Business Development and Strategic Marketing, championed the idea of a 'Knowledge Lab' and helped to secure the multi-million dollar funding it required. The Knowledge Lab concept was of a research and development centre that brought together the skills of NCR with those of about twenty of the world's main banks. The goal was to explore the future possibilities for technology and consumer behaviour in a partnership.

On 3 October 1996, NCR unveiled its new Knowledge Lab. Built at a cost of $10 million, it was intended to be an extended resource for the banking industry at a time when it is on the brink of a fundamental restructure.

Changes both in technology and consumer behaviour are shifting the familiar landscape in which banks once operated, blurring industry demarcation lines and creating new channels to the consumer. Technology is dismantling barriers to entry and the industry is being opened up to a wide range of non-traditional financial services providers. Banks and financial institutions are therefore having to rethink the very tenets of their business. To quote Senior Vice President Per Olof Loof, 'We need to see the future before it arrives . . . and do it faster than the competition.'

The partners are from a wide geographical spread and NCR has brought in people such as Dr Stephen Emmott; he became the Lab Director, having previously been head of research at Bell Labs electronic commerce department. Other lab staff come from various disciplines: biophysics, computer software design, psychology, economics and neuroscience; in total, there are about twenty full-time staff members. They do 'real' research and all the knowledge of the Lab is shared with their partners – the customers who are involved in and contribute to the Lab. Their particular interests are future technologies, artificial intelligence and consumer behaviour. In concept, the Knowledge Lab has strong similarities to MIT's Media Lab in the US, which combines academics and business partners to research the future of communication and media.

The Challenge

Senior management at NCR saw the need to adjust to a rapidly shifting business environment where customer expectations about banks – what they can do and what they should do – were being set by outsiders.

In addition, social and economic pressures mean that consumers are becoming ever more demanding, more sophisticated, more value-orientated and less differential. They are taking their expectations from one sector and applying them to others.

To succeed in this new territory, NCR saw the need to rethink the future from a fresh perspective, unburdened by the baggage of the past. Preconceptions about retail banking, its business and its technical requirements, had to be discarded by the entire industry in an effort to compete successfully in an uncertain future environment.

Knowledge sharing throughout the entire industry was essential if the banking industry was not to enter a slow, long-term decline. The Knowledge Lab stands as a visible mechanism to mobilise all the industry know-how, technological expertise and human resources at its disposal.

What Happened?

In early 1996, Per Olof Loof came up with the idea of a Product Demonstration Centre for NCR but Kicki Wallje-Lund suggested it would be better to have something unique; it seemed that everyone had a product demonstration centre. The Knowledge Lab was born from this thought-process.

The first quarter of 1996 saw the organisation propose a Mission Statement for the Knowledge Lab, together with a budget allocation and facilities planning. The period from March to June saw action towards achieving the mission statement, while the following quarter concentrated on logistics and planning for the grand opening.

Management at NCR readily acknowledge that an organisation-wide strategy was not in place before the opening of the Knowledge Lab. It was only in 1997 that NCR was able to involve the banks in the range and variety of collaborative research for which the Knowledge Lab was intended.

A typical project would be one looking at 'data mining', extracting and analysing information from a data warehouse. Data mining can help predict consumer behaviour. Currently, all approaches are based on classical statistical models, but the Lab has looked at applying Bayesion mathematics, which offers a new approach to prediction. The falling costs of computing are making the use of this statistical approach more affordable.

The partners are active in the project; they contribute people, funds and source data from which to work. This type of research could not be attempted by any one bank, but together it is possible. The results are impressive, predicting customer profitability, propensity to buy and retention rates.

Results

In a recent interview, strategist C.K. Prahalad stated that the next decade will be more about synthesis than analysis. With this in mind, NCR has taken active steps in addressing the changing business needs of its consumers, the retail banking industry. The stated ambition for the Knowledge Lab was to be a 'world-wide hub for learning and discovery', and the organisation is now in a position to use the Lab to harness the substantial intellectual capital available in the industry.

In Stephen Emmott's view, the biggest successes of the Lab have been in attracting so many of the world's top banks, carrying out innovative research and in strengthening NCR's customer relationships.

There are four workshops for partners each year but, increasingly, the knowledge sharing is taking place between partners independently and between partners and the Lab staff on an ongoing basis.

Key Learnings

Consumers are taking their expectations from one sector and applying them to others.

The next decade will be about synthesis, rather than analysis.

Most organisations start knowledge-sharing initiatives within the confines of the organisation itself. NCR has challenged traditional banking perspectives on strategy and competition with its creation of the Knowledge Lab.

The Lab is NCR's answer to the notion that banking – not banks – are vital to a modern economy. To quote Kicki Wallje-Lund once more, the lab 'provides an opportunity for sharp minds to meet and cross-pollinate'.

Contact Details

Dr Stephen J. Emmott
Director, The Knowledge Lab
Tel: +44 (0)171 723 7070
World Wide Web: http://ncr.knowledgelab.com
E-mail: knowledge.lab@unitedkingdom.ncr.com

Royal Mail Consulting

Background

The Post Office is split up into four separate entities:

- Post Office Counters
- Royal Mail
- Parcelforce
- The Subscription Services Ltd (this part of the business is responsible for telemarketing, also known as the company that processes our TV licences)

Royal Mail Consulting is an arm of the Royal Mail. Internally, it acts as an in-house consultancy to the Post Office. Externally, it is a specialist consultancy to international postal services, especially in Eastern Europe, the Far East and Africa. It has approximately 1,000 people operating from offices in London, Chesterfield and Swindon.

Royal Mail Consulting operates across the entire supply chain; it also provides tailored distribution processes and mailing solutions for large customers, such as National Westminster Bank. Mike Hall, Director and General Manager, sees the company's primary objective as applying 'world class post office knowledge to the postal value chain to maximise the business success of our clients'. Its associated aim is to be the 'number one consultancy in the global post office and related distribution market'.

Context

Royal Mail Consulting came into being in 1992. The catalysts for its birth were: growing competition in the world-wide postal service; the increased liberalisation of global postal services, and the new technology which often eliminated the need for companies to use hard-copy documents. At Royal Mail Consulting, management realised that the coming decades would bring profound changes upon all businesses, including the Post Office. However, the need for physical products will not disappear: faxes and electronic mail have contributed greatly to the decline in the use of paper, but paper documents, forms, applications and bills are still needed and, therefore, the postal service that delivers them will stay in business. In addition, it seems that the internet is a major contributor to a growing volume of physical mail and parcel delivery.

The postal service, as we know it, has come a long way since the message-relay systems of the ancient world. It has a pivotal role in everyday life, for both businesses and individuals. We take it almost for granted that a first-class letter will reach its intended addressee the following day. However, the Post Office also provides a range of services that have no direct connection with its traditional function of exchanging letters. In providing for the collection, transport, and delivery of letters throughout the country, the Post Office has established a network of post offices which extends into the remotest areas. The network provides an efficient banking service in areas where it would be uneconomic for a commercial or state bank to establish a branch office, and this means that social security benefits – such as pensions and family allowances – can be cashed at Post Offices anywhere in the UK.

The Challenge

Amid this increasingly complex business environment, the Post Office had to face the challenge of making 'people' expertise available within the organisation so that everyone would benefit. Senior management recognised that, to gain competitive advantage, there was an urgent need to manage the knowledge assets of the organisation better. Systems are merely the enablers; knowledge only becomes power when shared, and it is this sharing which leads to innovation and new product development.

Royal Mail Consulting was to become the knowledge business of the Post Office. Its objective was to customise knowledge for the postal and distribution market. Jim Marsh, Director of Knowledge in Royal Mail Consulting is very clear about the organisation's role in maintaining and enhancing the knowledge that resides within the business. This knowledge is unique to the Post Office, and Royal Mail Consulting 'aims to ensure that its people and teams are flexible, highly motivated and possess the knowledge, skills and experience necessary for business success'.

What Happened?

In 1993, Royal Mail Consulting was split up into 23 practitioner groups based on functionality and defined by expertise. The company has moved from being organised hierarchically to becoming a 'spider's web organisation'; it uses networking to mobilise its competencies. Consultants now find themselves working on several assignments at any one time; usually they manage one project and are heavily involved in others.

Jim Marsh, as Knowledge Director, has the task of ensuring that knowledge management is embedded into the structure of Royal Mail Consulting; he must also keep the consultancy abreast of external developments in the field. The organisation maintains various links with business schools and universities, consultancies and associates of the organisation, to help keep the company up-to-date. Benchmarking is widely used to enable and develop a 'knowledge culture' within Royal Mail Consulting.

Trust and empowerment are key drivers of the management style. However, the loose structure does not take away the accountability of the practitioner groups. Once a project or assignment has been completed, the project team is responsible for logging the results on to a Lotus Notes database; only then is the billing for that project allocated to the practitioner group.

The organisational structure requires that each consultant's time is 70 per cent billable in a twelve-month period. The remaining 30 per cent can be used for internal development, training, process improvement or innovations – anything that will add to the professionalism of that person and, ultimately, the organisation. Royal Mail Consulting provides support for the professional development of its staff by sponsoring MBAs, MScs and other professional qualifications.

Results

The 70:30 split of billable consultancy time has served to high-light the organisation's commitment to its 'Investors in People' programme. It has also created a roadmap to create individual strategies which, in turn, lead to an organisational strategy. However, the onus is very much on the individual; s/he is responsible for his or her personal development.

An in-house publication, *The Journal*, allows consultants to contribute articles on a wide range of subject areas, providing simple yet identifiable proof of the organisation's commitment to the concept of a 'learning' organisation. Royal Mail Consulting realises that people are judged not only by their skills and knowledge, but also by their reputation. With this in mind, it openly encourages consultants to present to both internal and external audiences. It also holds a 'Knowledge fair' where the remarkable leading edge products and projects that it produces are viewed from a 'knowledge perspective'; what knowledge did they use? What knowledge did the company gain from this activity?

Key Learnings

Shared knowledge leads to innovation and new product development.

Ensure knowledge is retained and preserved at the organisational level.

The most important realisation that Royal Mail Consulting has come to is that much of the downsizing of the 1990s would be better termed as 'dumbsizing'. As many organisations have come to realise – to their cost – the redundancies and lay-offs of the last decade have led to knowledge literally working out of the door. Many companies have suffered in this way, and the Post Office is no exception.

Royal Mail Consulting sees the deployment of its knowledge as key to its strategy of producing innovative products for existing and emerging markets. The Post Office avoids cases of 're-inventing the wheel' and tries to ensure that knowledge is retained and preserved at an organisational level, rather than the individual level as in so many organisations.

Contact Details

Jim Marsh
Director of Knowledge
Tel: +44 (0)171 320 7479

SmithKline Beecham

Situation

SmithKline Beecham Consumer Healthcare, the consumer arm of the pharmaceutical company, accounts for around one third of the entire company's turnover. It has a range of global and local brands, including names such as Panadol, Tums, Nicorette and Aquafresh.

The Challenge

One of the challenges for SB Consumer Healthcare was how to share knowledge and best practice among a large number of countries. How could they bring knowledge together and then ensure that all markets had access to it?

They decided to start by sharing knowledge about one brand that needed to be sold in far more markets than it was currently. With that goal in mind, SB embarked on a project lasting six months to gather, evaluate, organise and communicate everything valuable that the main markets knew about the brand.

A brand guide was initially in the early '90s a printed ring binder organised into key marketing areas such as advertising, product details, packaging, market research and regulatory issues. The guide was a managed version of what SB knew about the brand, as a subsidiary goal was to help focus and tighten the brands identity in all markets. Each page was organised like a 'windows' environment before Microsoft Windows was born. This allowed the knowledge to be communicated in small chunks with effective use of icons.

What Happened

The guide was applauded by all markets who either sold or wanted to sell the brand as the first time that people had formally shared knowledge about the brand, its history and its opportunities. It also helped forge a 'community' of people all working on this brand. Simply giving people some contact details for colleagues in other countries was unheard of and new contacts were made.

The guide was given to people at workshops run by SB in different markets, so that instead of simply receiving the knowledge, brand teams were able to investigate the resource while also thinking about the market locally and how the target audience responds to brands.

It is interesting to note that while this was a clear example of Knowledge Mobilisation, its goal as viewed by SB was to build the brand business globally by giving a boost to existing markets and also enabling new markets to launch the brand. Knowledge Mobilisation was the means to reach that business goal. As has been discussed earlier, Knowledge Mobilisation that has a clear business objective and strategy is a clearer and more actionable proposition for managers.

The success of this first knowledge-sharing venture encouraged many other parts of SB to follow a similar path, building new ideas and ingredients into the 'communication package' as different brands were addressed.

The Results

The media used for communicating knowledge have gradually evolved over the four years since the Knowledge Mobilisation work started, to now include Lotus Notes, CD-ROM and Intranet. However the overall development and communication process remains the same.

Some instances of brand knowledge sharing have worked better than others due to the level of interest in the brand across SB. Some brands have more markets and are more important to their markets than others. Consequently, some brands have benefited in greater terms than others from the process.

There have been improvements in brand profitability and many non-measurable savings in people's time due to not having to 're-invent the wheel'. It has also helped develop increased levels of cross-border contact between marketing people and has also extended communication between other functions such as R & D, regulatory, sales and manufacturing.

Key Learnings

The main learnings are that Knowledge Mobilisation gains from having a clear business goal for it to work best. Managers allocate their time based on what contributes most directly to their business performance and Knowledge Mobilisation is a means, not an end.

There are unseen spin-offs from the process in forging better contacts across businesses that are not expected but bring rewards nonetheless in increased sharing of experience and time savings.

A matrix management approach to knowledge was actually easy to start and relatively inexpensive, showing that Knowledge Mobilisation does not have to take a year in planning and a million dollars to get going.

One frustration has been that people want knowledge to be 'real time' or as near as possible. Print does not achieve that but electronic systems offer the potential to do so. However, an Intranet web site needs to be maintained and updated and this requires people to do that job. Also, while an intranet site is terrific for much reference information, it is not an environment suited to reading and in-depth learning. So a combination of electronics and supporting print is the ideal combination.

Contact Details

Elaine Macfarlane
Director of Consumer Healthcare Communications, Smithkline
Beecham Consumer Heathcare
Tel: +44 (0)181 975 2000
E-mail:elaine.macfarlane@sb.com

TEG

Background

TEG, formerly known as The Empowerment Group, is a London-based internal communication consultancy. The company works on global projects with multi-national clients, using communication to enable people to work differently and so improve business performance. It uses various different kinds of media – print, electronic, video, audio, workshops etc – to do this. The company's aim is to enable people to change the way they work by mobilising the power of internal communication.

The company consists of six full-time people and a similar number of associates, working from a single office. It is headed by Paul Miller, one of three TEG directors. The company has won several awards for its work, including three prizes from the International Association of Business Communicators.

TEG competes with a number of niche players in the field and also with larger management consultancies. The area of communication consultancy is a fast-moving field; the rate of pace of change is being sustained by the advent of technologies – such as groupware and the internet – and also as a result of more decentralised and empowered organisations.

Paul Miller believes that TEG has to remain at the forefront of a dynamic field. The company's strength lies in its ability to address strategic as well as implementation issues: 'The implementation of communication-based projects is the difficult part and TEG does this well because we are not afraid of getting our hands dirty.'

TEG's motto is 'Inform, Involve, Empower'.

Context

Compared with some other of the case studies, the situation at TEG is different. The company did not have a specific problem that it was forced to address. As a small organisation advising large clients, TEG has had plenty of experience of knowledge sharing projects within large organisations. As a result, it is logical that TEG is constantly thinking about sharing what it knows internally and with its clients.

TEG's knowledge sharing capabilities are a source of competitive advantage. Paul Miller goes to great lengths to espouse the cultural importance of working together and collaborating: 'You cannot work in boxes.' TEG consultants work together physically; this is a characteristic of the business and, what is more, 'We do not use Lotus Notes to do it!'

The Challenge

How could an organisation like TEG create a formal knowledge sharing system in an organisation that was essentially informal? How could it develop people's capabilities in a continuous learning environment where people were expected to take on lots of responsibility?

TEG's challenge was to create a formal structure for knowledge sharing. The company decided to adopt principles from its client work and formalise these into knowledge sharing practices at 'home'.

What Happened?

TEG used an appropriate amount of technology to create an open computer network: everyone has access to each other's files and folders through a central file server. Consultants use the internet for research purposes and e-mail for client communication. ISDN links enable TEG to access CompuServe's research reports and receive artwork via the internet.

Voice-mail is a popular method of communicating with people when they are out of the office, but the key to internal communication, according to Paul Miller, is face-to-face contact. He recognises that this is made easier by the small size of the organisation, but nevertheless, everyone in the company is kept up-to-date about what is happening with the client work and also any internal developments.

External 'Empowerment Cafés' are held for clients and industry contacts where new ideas and concepts are exchanged, discussed and debated. Internal 'Empowerment Cafés' are held every six weeks to promote learning and development within TEG. Here experiences, thoughts and personal anecdotes are shared to broaden the scope of TEG's corporate wisdom.

'Fast Meetings' are an addition to knowledge sharing at TEG. These allow quick updates and provide consultants, who may be working on-site, with the opportunity to touch base with their colleagues.

Every three or four months, TEG staff have an 'away day' to exchange ideas, and staff are encouraged to add opinions on internal developments, suggest initiatives and improvements. The content of a weekly internal meeting is captured and passed on to all full-time and associate staff and suppliers, thereby increasing the reach of knowledge sharing beyond the organisation's own boundaries.

Paul Miller stresses the point that knowledge sharing is a natural part and parcel of daily life at TEG; it is the norm rather than the exception.

Results

It is rare for TEG's clients to report confusion over what one member of the organisation has said, contrary to another. To Paul Miller, this is a sure sign that internally, communication channels are operating efficiently. There is a high level of awareness of where each consultant is and what he or she is doing. This enables the company to avoid wasting time and money through duplication and misunderstanding.

Ease of access to staff members is facilitated by the small size of the company, but also by a collective responsibility to respond to each other, to clients and to suppliers. The system of extended project teams means that no single person has total responsibility for the entire project. There is much overlap which ensures that, if people are away, the project will not come to a grinding halt. So, although a consultant retains ownership of a project, he or she is not in complete control of it and must rely on the team for its ultimate success.

Key Learnings

The rate of organisational change will increase as a result of decentralised and empowered organisations.

Knowledge sharing can be the norm, rather than the exception.

Knowledge sharing is essentially a new concept for most organisations. The idea of changing the way you work regularly is also a new concept: organisations need to be malleable; people are capable of changing processes to adapt to a 'new' organisation.

There is no substitute for talking. There is a lot to be said for working together, even if people often spend considerable periods of time in remote locations. The human element of business processes is not merely a link in the system, it is a key driver that ensures the smooth operation of any business.

A key learning from project and personal appraisals has been the success of setting and evaluating objectives in the knowledge sharing area. It is important to challenge people who do not want to function in this way. A knowledgeable consultant who shares know-how is more valuable to an organisation than one that does not. It also allows the easy switching of consultants between projects.

TEG is confident that its people, and therefore its clients, are all the better for following the three guiding principles of 'Inform, Involve, Empower'.

Contact

Paul Miller
Managing Director
Tel: +44 (0)171 467 3950
E-mail: paulm@teguk.com
www.teguk.com

Thomas Miller & Co

Background

Thomas Miller is a transport insurance management company. It is based in the City of London with offices around the world. It has 500 staff in twenty-one locations: 400 staff are based in London; the other offices range in size from one to twenty-five people. Very small branches are usually established in a supplier's or joint venture partner's office.

Context

In 1990, the Chairman recognised the importance of making the connection between the needs of the business and the capabilities offered by information technology. With this in mind, Mark Holford, then a manager in the underwriting function, conducted a nine-month survey of the technologies that were potentially vital to the company's survival, or those that would provide Thomas Miller with a competitive advantage in a comparatively conservative industry.

His findings were presented to senior managers in 1991. Most were immediately interested. He had identified groupware communications and desktop computing amongst his 'key' technologies. The executives realised that the existing infrastructure was imposing considerable barriers to progress, and that there was an urgent need for a new approach.

The Challenge

As in most companies, the challenge for Thomas Miller was

cultural. Even more significant was the culture of the industry: the insurance business is steeped in tradition; companies in the City of London are renowned for their expertise in one area or field. The concept of Lotus Notes was going to 'blow open' the whole concept of sharing information.

The notion of sharing is now embedded into the culture of the organisation. The Value Statements of Thomas Miller include the objective: 'To value teamwork at all levels of the firm's endeavours and to want to share our information, ideas and expertise with others'.

What Happened?

In 1991, Thomas Miller created two new posts. Mark Holford was the first Group Director of Information (Jacqueline Rees took over in 1996); and there is also a Group Director of Information Technology. The rationale for having these posts is simple. The former role is, as the title suggests, very much focused on information for the business user. The latter has a technology directive, ensuring that the company is providing its users with the relevant information systems to support its business needs.

At Thomas Miller, there is now a PC on every desk. Each member of staff uses e-mail, and Lotus Notes has become the company-wide medium for knowledge sharing. Video-conferencing is now widely used for meetings between Thomas Miller staff and customers in remote locations.

Results

An information culture has flourished under three directives set by Mark Holford back in 1991:

1 Share your knowledge
2 Keep it up-to-date
3. Don't waste it!

There are no reward systems for sharing information. However, it has become clear that not sharing leads to isolation. Staff are tuned into the realisation that information saved on their hard-drives is better off on a Notes database where it becomes meaningful.

The Notes databases come under the watchful scrutiny of an Information Editor, who works primarily from home and is responsible for pushing team-members to maintain the integrity of the databases. This role ensures a level of data protection as well as maintaining an index which makes relevant information more accessible to users.

The company has a target of implementing two new Notes applications every three months. A useful new addition to the Notes system is the Miller Encyclopaedia. It includes references to the insurance business, Thomas Miller contacts and world wide web references and commentaries. The Miller Encyclopaedia can also be used by the company's clients.

Open plan offices reflect the sharing principles of the information culture, and a learning and information centre, headed by the group personnel director, or 'learning broker', is a physical manifestation of the concept of 'share it; don't waste it; keep it up-to-date!'

Key Learnings

Share the information on your hard-drive — make it meaningful.

Knowledge mobilisation is an on-going process: set realistic targets to keep the momentum going.

The drive for Notes came from the company's need for better information management. Data had to be turned into information; the information had to be captured; it had to be consistent, shared and available. To achieve this, Thomas Miller drew heavily on the expertise of underwriters, some of whom had nearly fifty years experience.

Notes fits neatly with the Chairman's vision of how the business should grow: it supports the company by enabling information to be managed coherently and systematically. The key, according to Jacqueline Rees, is for each organisation to manage its information 'appropriately'.

Contact Details

Jacqueline Rees
Group Director of Information
Tel: +44 (0)171 283 4646

12.
Finally . . .

If Only We Could Mobilise The Power Of What We Know . . .

These are early days for this new science (or art) of knowledge mobilisation. This book has charted some of the lessons learned so far, things to keep in mind and lots of experiences from those who have made a little progress. Keep in mind that in the early days of any emerging business change, there are bound to be mistakes and blind alleys – but that's how we learn.

In our work in this developing field, we must all try to keep things simple, practical and accessible. Keep a few points at the forefront of your mind:

- Start off with an area of knowledge that people really value
- Don't let the technology seduce you
- It's about people talking to each other
- Work with the 'community' throughout
- Different organisations and cultures require different approaches.

Good luck and in the spirit of the topic please and let me know how you are progressing. The TEG website contains our latest thinking on the subject and links into other useful knowledge mobilisation sites.

Paul Miller
Managing Director
TEG
2 Thayer Street, London, W1M 5LG
Tel: +44 (0)171 467 3950
Fax: 0171 467 3951
E-mail: paulm@teguk.com
www.teguk.com

References

Books & Articles

Davenport, T.H. & Prusak, L. *Working Knowledge* Harvard Business School Press: USA 1998

Drucker, P. *Managing for the Future* Butterworth-Heinemann Ltd: UK 1992

Harari, O. 'The Brain Based Organisation' *Management Review* June 1994

Hiebler, R. 'Benchmarking Knowledge Management' *Strategy & Leadership* March/April 1996

Houlder, V. 'The Power of Knowledge' *Financial Times*

Lank, E. 'Cafe Society' *People Management* February 1998

Manville, B. & Foote, N. 'Strategy as if Knowledge Mattered' *Fast Company* April/May 1996

Nonaka, I. 'The Knowledge-Creating Company' *Harvard Business Review* November/December 1991

Nonaka, I. & Takeuchi, H. *The Knowledge-Creating Company: How Japanese Companies Create the Dynamics of Innovation* OUP: UK 1995

Peters, T. *Liberation Management* Macmillan: London 1993

Prusack, L. 'The Knowledge Advantage' *Strategy and Leadership* March/April 1996

Quinn, J., Anderson, P. & Finkelstein, S. 'Managing Professional Intellect: Making the Most of the Best' *Harvard Business Review* March/April 1996

Stewart, T. 'Getting Real about Brainpower' *Fortune 27 November 1995*

Ward, A. 'Lessons Learned on the Knowledge Highways and Byways' *Strategy & Leadership* March/April 1996

About the Author

Paul Miller is the Managing Director and co-founder of TEG, a London-based internal communication consultancy that uses communication to enable people to work differently and so improve business performance. It specialises in helping large organisations to inform and involve their people in organisational change. TEG has won awards for business communication.

Paul Miller entered communication management consultancy after a career in national business journalism. He has consulted at senior levels within large multi-nationals on the practical use of communication tools and materials to bring all types of organisational change to life. He is a graduate in Law and Chairman of the International Association of Business Communication Industry Group in the UK.

Since 1992, TEG has been a pioneer in the practical use of communication in organisations using a range of media. TEG has developed practical communication tools to help organisations mobilise knowledge.

He is married with two daughters and lives in London.

Index